A Load of Bull
An Englishman's Adventures in Madrid

Tim Parfitt

MARAVILLA PRESS

First published 2006 by Macmillan.

First published in paperback 2007 by Pan Books, an imprint of Pan Macmillan Ltd.

This edition reissued and published by Maravilla Press 2024.

Copyright © Tim Parfitt 2006

Additional content copyright © Tim Parfitt 2024

The right of Tim Parfitt to be identified as the author of this work has been asserted by him in accordance with the Copyright, Designs and Patents Act 1988.

ISBN: 978-1-7393326-2-4

All rights reserved. No part of this book may be reproduced, stored in or introduced into a retrieval system, or transmitted in any form or by any means (electronic, mechanical, photocopying, recording or otherwise), without the prior written permission of the publisher.

A CIP catalogue record for this book is available from the British Library.

Cover design, Llorenç Perello.

Praise for *A Load of Bull – An Englishman's Adventures in Madrid.*

> '*Parfitt is no ordinary Englishman ... his light touch and neat line in self-deprecating humour perfectly suits this entertaining urban spin on the old tale of Brits having fun under the Spanish sun.*'
>
> — The Sunday Times

> '*Hugely entertaining memoir ... frequently laugh-out-loud funny.*'
>
> — The Daily Express

> '*A love letter to Madrid ... brilliantly captures a truly eccentric and hedonistic place.*'
>
> — The Daily Mirror

> '*A Load of Bull chronicles his Spanish experiences in often hilarious detail.*'
>
> — BBC Online

> '*Magnificent ... brilliant and moving, hilarious and truthful.*'
>
> — La Vanguardia

*This edition is dedicated to my parents,
for showing me Spain in the first place.*

Introduction

A Load of Bull was first published by Macmillan in 2006, and then as a Pan paperback in 2007. That first edition covered most of the years I spent living in Madrid, working for Ediciones Condé Nast and Spanish *Vogue*, starting in January 1988 and ending – because the publishers wanted the book to end on a 'high' – in summer 1994. I worked in Madrid for two more years, however. For this new edition, I have included five extra chapters (39-43) that cover that final period, and which were cut from my original book.

Chapters 1-38 are the same as published in 2006. Today, I am conscious about some of the 'laddish' text and passages objectifying women, but decided it would have been wrong to edit them. They reflect the period in which the book takes place. I hope you can accept and enjoy it – and that at times you will laugh out loud.

TP – February 2024

This is it.
This is what I'd always wanted.
This.

This house, this whitewashed finca, this rustic, split-level sprawl. The lawn, the pool ... that warm, aromatic, pine flavour of Spain. At last I could feel it. Why hadn't I come here first? Why had I put myself through nine years of trauma beforehand? I should have moved into an old Spanish farmhouse like this from the word go, then kept a diary about mules and incompetent plumbers, about trying to get a year's supply of olive oil from a dozen olive trees, or good wine from bramble-choked vines.

That's *how life abroad was supposed to be. Driving over dusty dirt tracks in a battered old Seat with the suspension made of blancmange, playing golf amongst the pine woodlands and majestic palm trees of some sporting oasis alongside the crystalline Mediterranean – or simply getting red, puffy and pissed on the* Costa.

There wasn't any other type of Spain, was there?
But there was.
There was Madrid.

1

'Where's the bedroom?'

'*Cómo?*'

'You know. Bed. Sleep.'

My Spanish was non-existent and my new home already a disappointment. On the Plaza de Colón, the Centro Colón was a plain-faced concrete block of dull grey, with its name set out in gigantic letters on the roof, lit up to neon-red at night. If you had a room overlooking the floodlit fountains of the Plaza de Colón itself, you'd be able to see the Christopher Columbus monument and several giant sculptures depicting his voyage and discoveries. If you had a room on the top floor, you'd be able to see the chic shopping street, Calle de Serrano, beyond the frenetic main arteries of the city, the Paseos of Castellana and Recoletos.

But I didn't have such a room.

It was Sunday, 31 January 1988, and my British

Airways flight had arrived at Madrid's Barajas airport at ten that night. Condé Nast Publications, my employers in London and the publishers of *Vogue*, *Tatler* and *House & Garden*, had sent me over on a ticket with a return flight valid for six months. But I was only to stay there for six weeks, they said. Six weeks maximum.

Whilst happily overdosing on *cava* on the plane, I'd convinced myself that the Centro Colón would be a luxury hotel. But the lobby reception was classic late sixties: beige and brown furniture, rubber plants in huge tubs, white PVC sofas, chrome sculptures and ornate, fake crystal chandeliers. It looked like a set from a *Pink Panther* movie. The lift smelt of Ambre Solaire inside, as if the previous occupant had just come in off the beach. But I was 600 kilometres from the nearest shore.

Half-pissed and ravenous, I was shown to a fourth-floor turquoise room – an *'apartamento'* – by a lanky, goofy-looking Spanish porter, who reeked of flowery cologne, and whose crusty handkerchief hung from his pocket.

I had followed him into what I had assumed was the turquoise living-room that would expand into a turquoise bedroom. So far, it was a large enough space with a modest round table in the middle with two chairs, a coffee table, a turquoise sofa, a tiny TV, a wardrobe with glass doors ornately decorated with turquoise curtains, and a smelly kitchenette. We'd passed the bathroom on our right as we squeezed in, so I knew where that was, but not only was there no sign of a bedroom, there was no sign of a bed. What *was* the Spanish word for bed? I'd suddenly lost all knowledge of the Spanish I'd tried to learn on my crash course in London with Lola, my lunchtime teacher. I put my palms together and pressed them to the side of my cheek – the feeble international sign language for bedtime.

'You know. Bed. Sleep.'

'Ah, *claro!*' exclaimed the porter. He dropped the luggage and fiddled with some clips on an enormous work of crap-coloured modern art on the wall. With a couple of clicks, it suddenly sprung down and transformed itself into a large single bed, taking up the whole space we'd just been standing in.

'There's the bed,' I pointed, unsure whether to laugh or cry. 'That's great. *Fantastico. Muchas gracias.*'

The porter sneezed very loudly, whipped out his caked handkerchief and blew his nose at length. He then spent a good ten minutes demonstrating how the bed could easily be flipped back up against the wall, if and when I ever needed it to. At one point, he started doing an impersonation of someone skiing. As he rocked and swayed from side to side making ski-pole actions, it occurred to me that maybe he was trying to explain how I should be careful not to touch anything on the sides of the bed if I ever entertained the idea of female company back at this *apartamento*. I shuddered at the thought of being suddenly propelled upside-down against the turquoise wall in the middle of the night while trying to get my leg over with some ravishing *Madrileña*.

'*Claro, claro,*' I kept saying – because I knew that *claro* meant, 'of course' – and Lola had instilled into me that it would always be better to agree with a *Madrileño* than attempt incomprehensible conversation. '*Gracias,*' I added, thanking him profusely for all his advice with as much as I could afford as a tip. I tried to usher him out – yet not before he'd squeezed and patted me a few times, taking me by the shoulder first, then grabbing a little bit more of me, one handful at a time, until I was just about carrying him on my back.

But finally I got him out of the room.

I was twenty-seven years old and alone in Madrid for six weeks.

Having quickly unpacked, I decided to go out for a stroll to stock up the tiny fridge. But suddenly – *oh, sweet Jesus!* – I got as far as the lift doors before marching swiftly back to my room. Tomorrow I had to be at the Spanish *Vogue* offices at eight in the morning. What seemed like a glorious and glamorous piss-up last November, when it was first mooted I come over, was now a petrifying reality. It had been great fun to be able to say that I was *being sent* to Madrid to help launch *Vogue* – but now that I was actually here, I was seized by a potentially catastrophic panic attack, of a kind well known for their instantaneous laxative capabilities.

No one back in London had understood why Condé Nast were launching *Vogue España*, even less why they'd sent me over to help.

'*Vogue* in Spain?' they'd snort. 'What for?' Surely there wasn't a fashion industry in Spain? What would Spanish *Vogue* feature? Fashion for matadors? High-waisted *toreador* pants with pink tights, cut-off *boleros* and flouncy blouses?

Worse still, what the hell was *I* doing there? I'd convinced myself and others that Condé Nast was sending me first-class to a five-star hotel in Madrid – but here I was with no view, no mini-bar and a bed that folded down from the sodding wall! No one had met me at the airport. Would Condé Nast have put Anna Wintour, editor of American *Vogue* and ex-editor of British *Vogue*, in a turquoise pit like this? Of course not. But then I wasn't exactly Anna Wintour, was I?

How, anyway, was I going to help launch a magazine in Spanish when I couldn't even communicate coherently with the hotel's porter? Well, I obviously wasn't. I felt like phoning Condé Nast, thanking them for the flight and the miniature *apartamento* and saying, 'Thanks, but no, seriously, I don't think I'm the right guy for the job. I just wanted to fly over for a little jolly, you know, have a night out on the town, see some sun, taste some *sangria*, try to get laid and then fly home. Thanks, anyway.'

But it was too late. I had to be there at eight in the morning or I'd never have a job in London to go back to. And tonight, I would stay sober, have an early night, then get up *pronto* to make sure I was at the offices on time.

As I'd promised myself to have a quiet night, the idea of invading the bars close to my hotel was a non-starter. I decided I would simply stroll down nearby Recoletos and look at them from the outside to get my bearings for another night. It was a clear, dry sky – the dark evening air not cold, but crisp and cool – with the noise and chat of human warmth emanating from the streets. Couples were strolling up and down, all wrapped up, but for an Englishman having flown in from freezing fog, this was a spectacularly mild evening.

Madrid immediately felt *safe* – open, generous and hospitable – and I could already witness the dark, tantalising beauty of the women sauntering by. In fact people were everywhere, all ages, sizes and shapes, all strolling along – almost waddling – and all chatting to one another with no sense of urgency at all. Whilst *I* thought it was late, anxious to stock up my fridge before an eleven o'clock curfew, it was obviously still early for everyone else. Whole families were still out – grandparents, parents, children, cousins and friends – all waddling along with their arms linked, some with toddlers still awake in pushchairs. *Toddlers still awake!* This didn't happen in England – not at this time of night, not on a Sunday. It was eleven o'clock, for heaven's sake. I mean, why weren't they all at home, depressed and bloody miserable, all watching Spanish *Songs of Praise*?

Not only were they still on the streets, but they all looked smart and friendly too, all greeting, hugging, patting and kissing one another. In fact, on that first evening in Madrid, at least two strangers edged past me on the street and in the foyer of the apart-hotel wishing me a good evening, with '*Hola! Buenas noches!*' To a Londoner, this was verging upon unlawful harassment.

The dress code looked conservative, though. Lots of navy-blue and bottle-green – with many of those Austrian-style 'Loden' jobs being worn like capes – and lots of fur coats, tweed jackets and even ties on this crisp Sunday night. And all these people waddling up and down seemed so relaxed and satisfied. They looked like they knew exactly where they wanted to live and remain: right *here* in the centre of Madrid – where there were literally hundreds of *Madrileños* simply strolling along, *paseando* at their leisure, enjoying their own charming city and the last hours of an unseasonably warm weekend.

I, of course, was walking too fast.

I realised quite quickly that I was overtaking everyone – but why, I couldn't tell you, other than my fear that everything was about to shut. I tried to slow down to the pace of those around me, but it still wasn't slow enough, so I occasionally stopped dead and looked around, giving everyone else a chance to catch up. Then I mistimed it all when I tried to cross the roads. I was *too* slow, unlike the locals, who obviously knew pedestrian crossings in Madrid meant bugger all.

Adjusting to this Spanish pace of life was to become a recurrent problem for me: knowing how to pace myself and go slow – then knowing when it was the right time to party and go fast. I had much to learn.

Madrid immediately seemed physically more Latin, more 'Spanish' than anything I'd ever imagined. Here, in the capital city that night, not just in the architecture that I could see, not just on the faces of the people *paseando*, but in the air and the whole atmosphere, too – *this* was real Spain.

Lola had recommended the Gran Café de Gijón and the Espejo – both a short stroll along Recoletos from the Centro Colón. She had been quite specific about the Gijón. As I was 'in publishing and all that stuff', she'd said that the Gijón, Madrid's most famous literary café, was a must. It first opened in 1888 and was usually referred to as one of Hemingway's old haunts, although Lorca, Picasso, Miró and Dalí had all downed a few in there at one time or another. It was one of the last cafés in Madrid to hold *tertulias* – an informal gathering of artists and intellectuals waffling on passionately about a specific topic or two. As I gazed in from the street across the popular window seats, I could see the nicotine-stained walls decorated with framed sketches and small paintings – while the waiters wore white tunics with red epaulettes, fussing over the *Madrileños* still sitting at marble-topped pedestal tables, enjoying the evening's nightcaps.

With the empty fridge back at the turquoise *apartamento*, however, I was more in search of a convenience store than a literary debate and exotic *tapas*. Besides, in my nervous state, I thought it would be prudent to eat something I recognised. I needed to buy some milk, bread, fruit, ham, eggs, cheese, chocolate and beer – even a Mars Bar would have helped – anything at all to soak up the airline *cava*. But as this was one of Madrid's central boulevards, there weren't any corner-shops or late-night mini-markets – and especially not at the Gijón.

I finally found a large cafeteria-patisserie under the Centro Colón apart-hotel itself called the Riofrio – which translates to 'cold river', and which just about sums it up. The Riofrio had very little atmosphere but rows of bench seats and stools encompassing a wide central bar area, with the delicatessen and patisserie near the door. Here, as I discovered was the case in many Madrid patisseries, they'd adopted the slowest and most complex packaging and payment methods known to man – especially a now famished and dehydrated Brit on a Sunday night. I queued to get attention as *Madrileños* eyed me curiously from all angles, then asked the girl behind the counter if she had any food – or at least bread.

'*Croissants, si,*' came the reply.

I opted for a pile of croissants, and with further pointing and nodding also managed to locate some cheese, ham, fruit and cans of '*ther-bey-tha*', the classic pronunciation of *cerveza* as practised on numerous occasions with Lola – and which now tested the patience of the poor girl in the paper hat behind the counter.

'*Fantastico*,' I thought. But – oh, no – not so fast. I first had to go to a different counter to pay and receive a little ticket – and then I had to take the little ticket over to another counter and wait while the croissants were neatly gift-wrapped.

I didn't need them gift-wrapped but they were going to be gift-wrapped, whether I liked it or not. Minutes passed while I watched, drooling, as the croissants were placed on a little triangular carton which was then folded very cleverly upwards and inwards, before ornate tissue paper was wrapped around and neatly tied up with a bow, topped off with a little rosette sticker.

Back in the *apartamento*, I ripped open the packaging and looked for something to cut up and peel the fruit. Nothing. After an insane, Spanish-dictionary-aided phone call down to the reception desk, the skiing porter returned with my kitchenette utensils: one fork, one knife, one spoon, one plate, one bowl, one saucepan, one glass and one corkscrew. It was too late. I'd already scoffed the lot.

I hardly slept at all that night. It was a foretaste of things to come.

2

I had discovered very quickly during my classes with Lola, that like most English-speakers, I had a major problem pronouncing Spanish words that contained a number of letter *r*s – and especially double *rr*s. I tried too hard to roll them, so much so that they often became *w*s. As *w* doesn't really exist in the Spanish alphabet, few Spaniards ever understood what the hell I was talking about. So a name like Rodrigo Rato, a Spanish politician (I like to think of him as Roderick Rat), would always come out of my mouth as Wod Wigo Wato – for all I know, he could have been the President of Japan with a name like that.

I knew what I was supposed to do. I needed my tongue to strike my alveolar ridge several times. But before you can do that, you first have to open your mouth wide, as though you're going to say, 'Oh'. You then have to position your tongue so that it lays straight, touching neither the top nor the bottom of your mouth. Then you need to bend the front half of your tongue and place the tip slightly behind where you normally put it to pronounce a *t* or an *n*, lightly touching the flat plain between your teeth and the canyon where your tongue would normally and quite happily sit, and *then* you need to quickly tense it, exhale forcefully, and allow it all to flap and vibrate against your mouth. But not too loosely or you end up with a sort of dribbly whistle.

So 'number three, Serrano Street', or 'Serrano, *tres*' in Spanish – the office address for *Vogue España* – was always going to be a tricky one. The first few times I tried it, after carefully preparing my tongue to trill against my alveolar ridge, I'd bravely attempt a monumental '*SeRRRano tRRes*' but it always came out as a slurring, frothy 'Sir Rhino Twes' – much to the bewildered stares of taxi drivers.

'*Quien?*' they'd say. Who the hell was Sir Rhino Twes?

'Sir Rhino,' I'd persist.

'*Thurbano?*'

'*Si*, Sir Rhino,' I'd say, pleased that they finally understood the street. But then they'd ask me to repeat the number. '*Twes*,' I'd spit, holding up three fingers and pushing them towards the taxi driver's face two or three times to ram the point home.

'*Veinte tres?*'

'*Si*, that'th it!' I'd froth and spray. 'That'th right. That'll do nithely.'

Twenty minutes later and I'd be dropped off not at

Serrano, 3, but at Zurbano, 23, the other side of town, where I'd pay and get out of the taxi. I never had the courage to try and redirect them to the real Sir Rhino.

Over the weeks, it took me a while to think of a plan. I'd mention the 'Sir Rhino' bit in the same breath as the nearby Plaza de la Independencia. This worked – *taxistas* soon latched on to the fact that it was Serrano and not Zurbano. But then came 'number *twes*'. I gave up trying to say it, to be honest, and simply changed it to *cinco*. It was easier to get out at number five and walk the extra block to get to work.

My name, too, proved impossible for most Spaniards to pronounce. A simple phone conversation would go like this:

'Can I speak to *so and so*, please?' I always started. '*Puedo hablar con* –?'

Everything was fine until they asked who *I* was before connecting me.

'*Soy* Tim Parfitt,' I'd say. 'I'm Tim Parfitt.' Simple enough, surely? No ... because I had to say it like a Spaniard. So I became *Teeem Parfeee*.

'*Dream Drarfeeeee?*'

'No.'

'*Tarfeee?*'

'No, not *Tarfeee. Teeeem Parfeeeeee* –'

'*Arfeee?*'

'Oh, for fuck's sake! Just tell them it's a "Paco" from *Vogue*.'

'*De donde?*' From *where?*

'*Bo-Gay!*'

Vogue was pronounced *'Bo-Gay'* in Spanish – the *v*s becoming mostly *b*s and the final *ue* always emphasised. So in *real* Spanish, I was:

Name? *'Teeeem Parfeeee.'*
Company? *'Bo-Gay.'*
Address? *'Sir Rhino Twes.'*
It was enough to drive you mad.

Luckily for me on that first morning, I didn't attempt a taxi ride to the office. I'd already calculated how near it was and I'd been plucking up courage ever since I'd woken up at five. By seven I'd already practised walking to Serrano, *tres*, and up three of the four flights of stairs to the reception, but then double-backed swiftly to Colón once I realised how near it was and how precarious I still felt. I *walked* up the stairs at Serrano because I hadn't been able to fathom out how the lift worked. It was one of those beautiful old mahogany and glass jobs with a little seat inside, very typical of old-style Madrid properties, but too risky a contraption for a trembling Brit at seven on a Monday morning.

My map had pointed me down from Colón along the Paseo de Recoletos to the Plaza Cibeles, the Trafalgar Square of the city, where demonstrators march to and where *Madrileño* celebrations end up at, mostly in the fountains after successful Real Madrid cup-ties. The statue in the middle, Cybele, is apparently a Graeco-Roman goddess of fertility, and she's surrounded by some of the city's most prominent buildings, including the Casa de Correos, the post office, an imposing, extravagant building for such a piss-poor postal service. Onwards along Alcalá I paced, up towards the five-arched Puerta de Alcalá, a mini Arc de Triomphe built by Carlos III.

As I hadn't worked out how to get breakfast at the Colón, I stopped off at a tiny café, the Cafetería Simpatía, just near the Puerta de Alcalá, where Monday-morning businessmen were already sipping *cafés* and chain-smoking fanatically. My first concern was ... why they didn't put their arms *through* their jacket sleeves. What was it with Spanish men? Why did they wear every garment as if it was a cape? Was it to keep their sword arms free?

Then there were the car stereos. When I saw one man holding his car stereo, I thought, that's odd, I've just seen another man doing the same thing. Then I saw two others, both clutching car stereos as well – so I assumed they'd all been to a car stereo sale. But it wasn't that. They were all carrying them because, if they'd left them in their cars, they'd be nicked. But how would you know who'd nicked one when they were all carrying them? As I stood on the side of the street waiting to cross (as you do a lot in Madrid), I peered in at people sitting on buses, clutching car stereos on their laps. How did *that* happen? Didn't they trust their own neighbours, wives or kids? Would they rather bring their car stereos to work than risk leaving them in their cars at home?

Serrano is in the affluent Salamanca area of Madrid and is the main fashion street – the Bond Street, the Fifth Avenue – where the designer shops are found huddled between one or two larger stores, endless jewellers and shoe-shops. Serrano, *'twes'*, itself was a beautiful old building, with a big black wrought-iron and solid glass front door, slightly arched, with a little white 'number three' on a blue tile placed at the top of it. There were tall shuttered windows with little half-balcony wrought-iron and stone window rails and, because the building stood on the corner of Serrano and the Calle de Recoletos, a semi-hexagonal foyer. A simple, shiny brass plaque outside said *'Vogue – 4° Izda'*, which meant fourth floor, left-hand door.

When I finally turned up again at quarter to eight following my seven o'clock practice-run, no one else was there, except the cleaner and the porter who looked at me as if I was as mad as a *sombrero*. After much finger-waving and pointing at watches to show how the hands moved around, I finally gathered that there wouldn't be anyone there at eight-thirty. After a few more shrugs, neither did it appear that anyone would be there at nine o'clock. In fact, it was more likely to be nine-thirty or ten – especially on a Monday morning.

So I had nearly two hours to kill!

I could have left a note to say that I'd turned up but no one was in, and then flown swiftly and safely back to London. I could have done with some extra sleep, or maybe found a good breakfast somewhere instead of more gift-wrapped croissants – but I simply settled on going back to the *apartamento* to start the whole day again. At nine-fifteen I reappeared at Serrano, *tres*, refreshed and raring to go, thanks to the two dress-rehearsals I'd already had.

This time I plucked up the courage to use the old lift, which rattled its way slowly up the central staircase to the fourth floor, and where a young shy receptionist finally greeted me in English, much to my relief.

'*Señor Parfeee?*' she said. 'From Engerland, *si?* I am Elena. *Hola!*'

I stood in the reception area, observing the neat glass shelving displaying worldwide *Vogues* and other Condé Nast titles while the young Elena tried to get her mini-switchboard working. Everything looked as if it was new and being tested: the switchboard, the typewriters, the highly polished wooden floor. There was a strong smell of fresh paint, and even Francisco himself looked new as he breezed into reception to welcome me.

Francisco Rodríguez, the Puerto Rican art director of the new *Vogue*, was a gangly, slightly nervous yet pleasant guy in his early thirties who wore National Health-style thick-rimmed spectacles. Thin, fairly tall, and with curly black hair, he wore an oversized blazer and a loud shirt undone at the collar with a big, loosely knotted floral tie. He had several earrings and a huge skull-and-crossbones ring on his finger – a cross between Woody Allen and Keith Richards – every bit the Puerto Rican art director.

'*Hola!*' he said, greeting me warmly. 'You're early!'

'Early?' I said. 'You said eight, right?'

'Welcome to Madrid,' said Francisco. 'Where eight o'clock means ten o'clock.'

He hugged me and slapped me on the back, then started to parade me around the individual offices where I was then also hugged, held, patted, squeezed and kissed by everyone. The double-greeting *Madrileño* always starts by squeezing and holding on tightly to your upper right arm with his own left hand while vigorously shaking your right hand – as if afraid that your arm is about to fall off or, worse, run off with his own. The kissing on both cheeks is done only by the women, thank God – and often on the first introduction. In Madrid, if you're not careful, it's quite easy to hold your hand out on being introduced to a complete stranger only to find yourself in a bear-hug swiftly followed by the kiss-of-life.

It was 1 February, and the launch date of *Vogue España* was set for 22 March. There was a TV commercial geared up for this date, and news-kiosks all over Spain had been reserved for a poster campaign. The launch issue was expected to be about 350 pages, with a print run of over 150,000 copies. This meant that the deadline for sending off all completed pages to the printer had to be 9 March – something I'd already worked out whilst Francisco had been ushering me down to my padded cell of an office. That's really why I'd been sent over for six weeks only. If by 13 March, the day I was due to be flying home, 350 pages were still hanging around at the *Vogue* offices, then there wasn't going to be any magazine launched on 22 March after all. One way or another, I would have either helped them or totally buggered it up.

The droopy-eyed Alfonso, the production manager, was totally unfazed. Alfonso had an Inspector Clouseau moustache, bushy eyebrows to match, and a permanently surprised expression on his face. He spoke no English at all and sat in the furthest office from everyone else – apparently by choice, but it really looked as if he had been banished there. So dark was his office that it was to eventually become the in-house 'dark-room'. He sat in a big brown corduroy armchair which had wheels and a handbrake and reclined like a dentist's chair, far from in keeping with the chic black leather and chrome in all the other offices.

Having brought me down the long corridor to introduce us, Francisco still hovered in the doorway, translating and politely explaining to Alfonso why it wasn't such a bad idea for me to have flown over. It was good to be reminded myself. I was there, he explained, to try and ensure that Condé Nast Spain followed the same publishing process Condé Nast London used, and to achieve the same quality.

To get us all off to a good start, Alfonso suddenly stretched his arms out wide and twisted his palms to face each other, as if holding up an invisible, long box. This, we were told, was his imaginary 'time-line'. As Francisco translated, Alfonso started to explain with simple karate-chop gestures along this time-line that, when a road or a building was made, the British started *here* and finished *there*. The Spanish, however, also *finished* exactly where (or when) the British finished (demonstrated by another karate-chop at the same point) *but* – and this seemed to be the key to it all – the Spanish started *here*, he beamed, karate-chopping *half-way* along the line, and *still* managed to get to the same end at the *same time* as the Brits!

When this confusing martial arts demonstration was over, Alfonso looked delighted with himself. Francisco and I glanced at one another in silence. I'd been in the building for twenty minutes and had already decided that Alfonso was an absolute nutter, albeit a lovely one. My job could have been all over and I could have left for London, there and then, simply by saying, 'Alfonso's right! You don't need me …'

Or I *could* have said, 'Alfonso's deranged! For crying out loud, get some work done! *Move it! Now! GO!*'

But then I probably would have been put on the next flight home as well. So instead, realising that I was already feeling hungry again, I decided to say: 'Well, I'll need to spend the day getting to grips with how Alfonso's planned all this …'

And with that, I hoped that I would at least be able to stay around long enough for some lunch.

3

'Try these,' Francisco said, once we all had a glass of chilled Viña Sol in our hands, as he passed me a plate of what looked like fried scampi – one of several dishes that he'd ordered for us all to pick at. I took one and started to chew.

'Like them?'

'Not bad,' I nodded. 'What are they?'

'Testicles.'

'Testicles?'

'Sheep's testicles,' he nodded. '*Criadillas*. A Spanish delicacy. Squeeze some more lemon on them. They're delicious.'

I did as he suggested and took another one, much to everyone's approval – but mainly because I was craving to just stuff *anything* into my mouth by the time we all went to lunch. It was half past two, for crying out loud. Not only had Alfonso and I ran out of all sign-language vocabulary by then, but we'd karate-chopped his time-line a thousand times and exhausted any possible compromise on his schedule, too. After my diet of croissants, I would have wolfed down an entire goat's penis and a flock of scrotums if they'd been placed in front of me, let alone a tiny, tangy testicle.

I say, 'by the time we *all* went to lunch', because there were nine of us in the end, including Alfonso, Francisco and myself. Firstly, Francisco had invited along the Spanish girls in the art department with whom I was supposed to work most closely – the blonde, short and permanently frowning art editor, Elvira, and the dark, shorter, permanently smiling art assistant, Paloma, who were both out of bounds, according to Francisco. They were accompanied by the two graphic designers: a thick-set Brazilian called Geraldo and a startled-looking Spaniard called Jacobo. There was also the blonde, Swedish Sonia, the fashion coordinator, who I guessed was in her mid-forties, gorgeous-looking, with very striking eyes, and who purred as she spoke. Then there was the mighty Mayte, who did *not* purr as she spoke. Mayte was the all-singing, all-dancing and all-shouting photographic editor and PA to Francisco. She spoke – no, she bellowed – in a big American voice when she wanted to, and had wild curly hair and a presence that dictated the whole atmosphere of the art department. When she greeted me, she did so by planting her vast, fat, wet lips far too near the corners of my mouth so that it felt like a bloody big snog rather than a gentle peck on both cheeks.

It was very kind of Francisco to invite so many people to my first lunch inauguration – but because they took ages to get their hats and coats on, then spent ages kissing one another, I feared the restaurant would be closed by the time we got there. In fact, while in the office with Alfonso, I got to the point where I assumed we'd already missed lunch. Either that or we were working through it. And either that or Alfonso was torturing me. It had been casually mentioned that Madrid ate late, but I never assumed it would affect or include me. *They'll* eat late, I thought. *I'll* be off round the corner at half-noon to the sandwich-bar – although I soon discovered that there weren't any sandwich-bars around any corners in Madrid. True *Madrileños* would never be found eating sandwiches at their desks for lunch. They expected a three-course meal, or at least the *menú del día*.

The old-fashioned-style restaurant that Francisco had chosen was actually just around the corner, in the Calle de Recoletos, which joined Serrano with the Paseo de Recoletos. There were numerous *cafeterías* and *tabernas* in this short street, some with window displays of baby pigs' heads garnished with lettuce and guarded with dusty bottles of Rioja. *Madrileños*, I'd heard, were very much into a hearty style of eating, and despite the city's influx of contemporary, international restaurants as part of its new image and late-eighties, euro-yuppie status, the locals invariably shunned the new venues in preference to their own home fare: lamb and pork roasts, or heavy stews with *chorizo*, black pudding, beans, lentils and too much garlic.

The restaurant was far from closed by the time we got there. The place only started to fill out at about three, with numerous round, short, moustached Spanish businessmen in shiny polyester checked jackets, all smoking their way from the bar to their tables, tossing the remnants of their *aperitivos* – the toothpicks, scrunched-up paper napkins, olive stones and prawn shells – onto the sawdust floor. They talked fast, gesticulating aggressively with their hands and elbows. Several times I was on the verge of interceding in what appeared to be a fight, only to find the people involved were actually having perfectly civilised discussions.

This first lunch was more like a banquet. We were swamped with further starter dishes to pick at, including cured ham, *manchego* cheese and roasted red peppers with tuna and crisp lettuce hearts. Then when a plate of what looked like larger fried scampi came round, I turned to Alfonso and tried to communicate with him in absurd sign-language – something about whether this was another plate of even bigger testicles.

'*Cómo?*' he exclaimed, and far too loudly for my liking. '*Cojones grandes?*'

The others stopped talking amongst themselves and looked across.

'You just ask Alfonso if he has big testicles?' grinned Francisco.

'*Do* you have big testicles, Alfonso?' purred the sexy Sonia.

This wasn't a good start. I hadn't expected lunch to be like this. I'd expected an outside terrace restaurant somewhere in the shade, with the sound of a softly strummed Spanish guitar, perhaps, and Gypsy women pressing carnations and bunches of rosemary on passers-by. I'd expected stunning Spanish waitresses with frills and flowers in their hair. I'd pictured horse-drawn carriages with drivers resting under orange trees, laden with fruit. I'd dreamt of the scent of jasmine and geraniums flooding narrow streets, cobbled and whitewashed ... and shady patios lined with coloured *azulejo* tiles where old ladies clucked among the ferns, selling ... OK, I didn't know what they'd be selling, maybe fans and castanets, or something like that. But instead, here I was in central Madrid, in a dark, smoky, fag-end-infested *taberna*, ploughing my way through another plate of fried bollocks. I was suffering a *Madrileño* executive's long, long, *long* lunch – the city life of Spain. There wasn't an olive tree, golf course or Moorish palace in sight.

'*Hombre!*' shouted Alfonso, finally understanding my sign-language query. 'These aren't bollocks, they're croquettes,' he said, with Francisco translating.

Last night I'd been hurrying along the streets in fear of an eleven o'clock curfew, and now here I was again, constantly looking at my watch, over-conscious that we were all still sitting there at gone four. I held back the urge to scream, 'Come on, finish your testicles! We've got work to do, for God's sake – you haven't got time to sit around chewing genitalia!' I needed to change my British body-clock, but for months, if not years, a day didn't pass by without something being obviously not synchronised for me in this frenetic, restless city.

Madrileños, it seemed, tucked into big lunches, often slept until six or seven, then got up and *stayed* up. Locals took early-evening strolls along the *paseos*, but they rarely went out for dinner before ten – and, if meeting for drinks, not until eleven or midnight. But I didn't yet *know* that. So, on another occasion, when Francisco and Mayte suggested they collect me at ten o'clock from the Centro Colón one night, I assumed it was for a nightcap. In fact, I was even offended that we *weren't* going for dinner. I took my revenge by having a slap-up room-service meal alone in my *apartamento* at eight, polished off a bottle of wine, and by ten o'clock I was ready for bed. When they finally turned up at the hotel at ten, saying, 'We've booked a table for half past,' I didn't have the courage to tell them what I'd been up to for the past two hours. Instead, I waded my way through another three-course meal. Our feast ended well after midnight – and *then* we went on for that nightcap in some backstreet music bar. By the time I was back at the *apartamento*, I'd dined twice and drunk four times as much as I should have. I was to rapidly put on weight, suffer from no end of stomach heckling and wake up most mornings with blurred vision and a mouth tasting like the inside of matador's jockstrap.

Anyway, when we did all shuffle back to the office at half-four after that very first lunchtime feast –

overfed, rosy and mischievous – I noticed we were still only the first back – apart from what now appeared as the pale, forgotten, undernourished Elena still studiously manning the silent telephones and vacant reception.

Leaving Alfonso to meditate in his dark cell, I spent time with Francisco in the editorial department in the afternoon, trying to understand what the first edition was going to be featuring, what photos were available for various articles, and whether any pages were ready to be sent to the printer. There were none.

Ana Puértolas was the 'acting editor' for the first edition of Spanish *Vogue*. Ana was in her mid-forties, bespectacled, bookish and laid-back, not a stereotypical *Vogue* fashion-victim at all. She introduced me to her team seated in the adjacent open-plan area – two senior sub-editors who were the real workers – the loud, round, mumsy Jacinta and the dark, sharp, sparkling Zulema. Then there was Laura García Lorca, too – the niece or great niece (or so I was told), of the Spanish poet Federico García Lorca, who was assassinated at the beginning of the Spanish Civil War. Laura was in her early-thirties, suitably romantic-looking, with pallid features highlighted by raven hair. She looked permanently stressed and overworked. She spoke several languages and for that reason had been inundated with most of the work, juggling an impossible dual-role of features editor with fashion editor. She'd been burdened with not only most of the interviews and features to write, but most of the picture research too, as well as all the captions to the fashion-shoots. She chain-smoked indefatigably as she followed Francisco and I around each department, helping out as an interpreter – possibly looking for a glimpse of how I might have been able to help her out of the maze that she was in.

With both Francisco and Laura translating, Ana explained what had been commissioned for the first issue, pointing at some miniature layouts pinned up on the wall. I noticed they were planning as an introduction for the launch a few collage-style pages of Spain as seen through the eyes of other *Vogues* in the world – and I recognised images of Dalí and Picasso, and made polite, 'Spanglish' comments like, 'That looks *fantastico*,' and, 'Should be *bueno*,' but most of it was alien to me. Then when I asked about the cover, they looked at me as if I was nuts.

'*Qué?*' asked Ana. As they all whispered to one another, I heard Ana murmur in Spanish, 'The cover? *Already?*' Maybe I shouldn't have asked – maybe it was far too early for them to realise the magazine might need a cover.

'Oh, we're not quite sure yet,' mumbled Francisco. 'But we're working on it …'

When they led me down to the fashion department, I noticed that the staff all looked excited yet fraught in the way that only fashion assistants know how to pull off. Amidst the jumble of designer bags and shoe-boxes, and squeezing between the rows of clothes-rails and packing-cases, I got introduced to the pert María, the fashion director, as well as her three stylists – the blonde Cecilia, the petite Helena and shy Belén, as well as the punk-looking 'booker of models', Sara, whose style would have looked a decade out of place in London, but who obviously felt very trendy in late-eighties Spain. It looked like a fun department, though, what with the loopy photography editor, Ugo, who also breezed in and out, peering down to greet me. That was a total of six fashion staff – roughly a tenth of the team that produced American *Vogue* every month.

'And the answer is *no*,' Francisco suddenly said, before I could ask anything at all, as I was busy still admiring María's nipples. 'There aren't any fashion pages that have been shot yet, let alone ready to send off to the printer, in case you were about to ask …'

'But we're ready to go,' promised María, as her dream team frantically finished packing trunks and strapping up suitcases ready for a glamorous shoot on some exotic location.

I wished I was joining them.

I had yet to meet Luis Carta, the man who'd suggested I come over and help out in the first place. According to his marvellously round, matronly secretary, María Teresa, who spoke good English, Luis would be back shortly. In the meantime, on our way back from the fashion department, Francisco introduced me to

Giovanni – Prince Giovanni de Borbón Dos Sicilias – *El Principe*.

'Old' Spain.

It would seem that every Condé Nast office in the world had a resident prince on the payroll, and Spain was no exception. Someone who could open doors and convince the unwilling to be interviewed and the inaccessible to have their homes or daughters spread across the magazine's glossy pages – and who could double up as a glorified society editor on the magazine's masthead. Giovanni was born Jean Maria Casimir Prince of Bourbon-Two Sicilies in Warsaw in 1933, and became Giovanni once his family emigrated to Italy. When Francisco introduced me to him, he told me that Giovanni's late father was the current King of Spain's uncle. He also then told me that when poor Giovanni was a toddler, he was pushed forward at a ceremony to present a bouquet to Adolf Hitler. So Giovanni obviously had a few stories to tell.

In our brief introduction, though, it was not explained to me quite why Giovanni was *here*, inside, working on a fashion magazine in Madrid, and not over *there*, outside, waving to the crowds, if you know what I mean. I gathered that he had prime responsibility for nothing more than the recipe page of the forthcoming Spanish *Vogue* – and that he was a former employee of Brazilian *Vogue*. Giovanni did, however, look as regal as you can get. He had the long Bourbon aristocratic forehead, nose and teeth, all of which went on forever, and he was crowned with neatly trimmed, swept-back silver hair. He was tall, immaculately attired and sat at a modest round table hidden at the back of the reception area with nothing on it other than a small typewriter, one or two pencils, the *International Herald Tribune*, a cookery book, and a couple of reference books such as *Debrett's* and *Who's Who*. He spoke any language you wanted him to – Spanish, Portuguese, Italian, French, German, Polish or Russian – although he spoke to me, thank God, in perfect English, tinged with an American-Italian accent. And the very first thing he said to me was:

'Now tell me, dear boy, why on earth would you leave England for Spain?'

Before I could reply, however, Francisco introduced me to a contrasting vision of 'new' Spain who had swiftly appeared in the shape of the manic commercial director, a frightening José Manuel Sanchez Palomares. He wore a tight-fitting snazzy T-shirt under a brown jacket with beige flannels and a white belt, from which jangled a bunch of keys. I hadn't seen a white belt for years. José Manuel seemed to know very little English at all, but what he did know, he spoke with such a sales-pitch excitement that I was swept along. He greeted me effusively, slapping and hugging me (I was totally bruised by now), then guided me away from Giovanni, almost symbolically, as if guiding me away from the 'old Spain', and across the reception area into his modern, 'new Spain' office, where we stood in the open doorway.

'Look!' he said, proudly making a sweeping gesture

at his walls. *Vogue* posters from the London office had been framed and hung around his office. There were numerous *Vogue* souvenirs and gimmicks lying all over his desk – baseball caps, T-shirts, pens, diaries, scarves and bags. He skimmed products that he'd been looking at for Spain, but then went to a cabinet and pulled out a long, thin red box from what seemed like several hundred stashed away.

'Open it,' he beamed, generously handing it to me.

It turned out to be a very large, blood-red fan – a Spanish *abanico* – that opened up to display the Vogue logo on the black handle. It was actually quite beautiful.

'We're giving them to all our friends, clients and advertising agencies,' José Manuel said. 'Take one. Take two. Take three. Take more ... for all your women ...'

Balancing them in my arms, I thanked him just in time before he suddenly went into his 'I-love-*Vogue*-but-Spain-is-different' routine.

'I love *Vogue*! I love Condé Nast! But Spain is different!' he cried.

I assumed he was pissed, but he wasn't.

There may be fifteen or so *Vogues* in the world now but the day I arrived in Madrid there were just seven. *Vogue* had been launched in the USA in 1892, Britain in 1916, France in 1921, Australia in 1959, Italy in 1965, Brazil in 1975 and Germany in 1979. Now *Vogue España* was to be launched in 1988, just thirteen years since Franco's death – which, in a sense, meant that it was probably still going to be a little conservative. But despite being under Franco right up until 1975, modern Spain, now portrayed to me in the shape of the mad José Manuel, still wanted its *Vogue España* to look and feel just like American or British *Vogue* – and *immediately*. Despite the fact that American *Vogue* had been going since the same year Franco was born, or that British *Vogue* had notched up sixty years before his death, José Manuel wanted it all right now.

Could *Vogue* just happen overnight? I wasn't sure, to be honest, but José Manuel kept saying that in Spain, it could. In fact, anything could happen in Spain, he said, because Spain was 'different'.

'I love *Vogue*!' he moaned, starting to thump a corner of his big glass desk that wasn't covered in corporate gifts. 'I love Condé Nast! But Spain is different!' He was going very red indeed.

'This – my – dream!' he cried, like a lunatic. 'Spain needs *Vogue*! Spain's time has come! I – will – sell – *Vogue* – in – my – country! We will be best! Spain is different! We will be better than British *Vogue*! Not tomorrow! Now! Because Spain is different!'

'Right,' I nodded. 'Well, that's jolly good, José Manuel. Well done.'

He then introduced me to some of his sales team who flitted in and out of his office. I made the mistake of asking simple questions about the advertising copy for the first edition. Silence and accusing stares. They had a thousand red fans to give away – but not a single advert ready to appear in the magazine.

From what I could see, I was beginning to wonder whether Spain, with its contrast of wannabe yuppies alongside the old Franco set, was quite ready for all this. Presenting new Spain with a new *Vogue* in the form of a corporate gift such as the red *abanico* fan – the cliché symbolising flamenco dancers and women in polka-dot dresses at bullfights – was a paradox too far. I wondered who would be guiding them to find the right balance. The answer came in the shape of a mammoth palm that suddenly came to rest on my shoulder. It was Luis Carta.

'Did he tell you what I said?'

It first appeared that Luis was speaking without opening his mouth, but when the words did come out in that Marlon Brando in *The Godfather* slow whine, well, believe me, you listened.

'Who?' I said.

'Francisco.' It came out in three very clear, almost hissed syllables: Fran. Sis. Co. 'Did. Fran. Sis. Co. Tell. You. What. I. Said?'

'Yes – *sí!*' I started. 'Yes, he did –'

'I said we'd be mad to not invite you over. Did he tell you that? I hope so. I told him to tell you that –'

'Yes, he told me,' I said. 'And thank you. Thanks for inviting me.'

From the word go, I could see that Luis Carta was someone very special. He was a big man in every sense of the word. Forget the way he spoke, he even *looked* like Marlon Brando in *The Godfather*, but with a well-trimmed, silver-white beard along the jowls and a dark moustache. Luis had immense presence – handsome, with green-brown, mischievously twinkling eyes and a knowing smile. His receding grey hair was slicked back over his ears, Italian-style, into a black curl at the back of his neck. His eyebrows were dark and alert, with a number of hairs spiralling out of control. Having emigrated from Italy to Brazil to seek his fortune, he had, in 1975, launched *Vogue Brasil*, adding *Casa Vogue*, a décor title, soon after. In 1987, he'd been asked by Condé Nast to prepare for the launch of *Vogue* in Spain, and thus the Spanish company had been formed. He was fifty-two, had been married three times and had apparently lost a fortune twice in alimony settlements.

Luis spoke to me in broken English but with the others in Spanish. As Francisco and Giovanni fired comments back at him, he smiled, and kept patting my shoulder with that mammoth palm before disappearing back to his office, with the final words: '*Hablaremos.*' We'll talk.

The afternoon dragged on with no apparent end in sight. Eventually, little Elena gave in and started to pack up her stuff at seven o'clock. She put the telephone switchboard on a direct line through to whatever department had agreed to answer it, and then left, followed by a steady trickle of employees right through to seven-thirty, eight, nine, even ten. The main rush hours in Madrid, I learned, were at two o'clock and four-thirty, getting *to* and *back from* lunch. No-one was in a hurry to arrive in the morning, nor leave at night.

By seven, however, I decided to make it look like I also had somewhere else to go. I'd collected enough notes for the day, armed myself with some schedules and was desperate for a beer. But I was unsure what was expected of me *after* work. I had no guide, no interpreter, no *chaperon* – no one even knew who I was. I hadn't expected an official tour guide, but nor had I given any thought to the fact that I was going to be alone. But then in Madrid, it's impossible to be alone for very long.

4

The food I'd sampled during the first office lunch was delicious, but I hadn't a hope in hell of ordering anything similar in the evenings, however hard I tried. I ended up eating things I could point to on plastic picture-menus in café bars, like *hamburguesas* or omelette *tortillas*.

My breakfasts consisted of further gift-wrapped croissants and coffee or hot-chocolate, followed by an overdose of Heathrow-stockpiled Rennies to get me through the day without exploding. But then Alfonso, at least for a few days, took over all my lunchtime plans to lead me on a tour of gastronomic delight. I soon realised that actually he was trying to kill me. There must have been a secret *Madrileño* code to deal with foreigners (or, if of the Anglo Saxon variety, '*guiris*') that said, 'If you can't beat them, feed them to death.' Alfonso, already aware of my delicate disposition, was trying to get me as fat and as pissed as possible, as fast as possible. There could be no other explanation for his hospitality. I'd have indigestive nightmares about it each night, featuring images of Alfonso towering over me with lambs' legs, pigs' heads and goats' testicles, trying to pulp me to death over my Ambre Solaire-stained turquoise pillow.

On the flimsy pretext of making late-morning business trips to our suppliers, Alfonso and I ended up in a top-class *paella* restaurant one day, and an Asturian one the next. Our *paella* feast started in a sophisticated manner with a glass of dry, cool *jerez* sherry. As the restaurant started filling out with spinning-top-shaped, smoking Spaniards, the red Rioja wine started to flow and we picked at a couple of starters – a large plate of the very best *jamón* and some grilled *esparragos*. Then it came, in an immense shallow pan – not just one *paella* but a huge combination of two, and enough to feed the Spanish Armada. Alfonso's plot was to murder me with a *paella* of prawns, clams, mussels, squid and chunks of eel, combined with an *arroz negro*, a delicious black rice dish cooked in squid's ink. The food was glorious and I was in heaven – though not the one Alfonso would have liked me to be in. We polished off the meal with lemon sorbets and ice-cold *pacharáns* – an aniseed-tasting liqueur from Navarra made from blue-black sloes, the fruit of the blackthorn tree, picked in late summer and immersed in spirits. An ice-cold *pacharán* is normally followed by another – larger – so after two more, we eventually made it back to Sir Rhino Twes at five – flushed and giggling, because we still couldn't understand a bloody word one another said.

No sooner had I tried to digest all this, however, than we set off to do it all again the next day – only with a different main course. Because I was still alive, Alfonso decided to try and finish me off with a *fabada* – the signature dish of Asturian cooking. Asturias is the green bit of northern Spain – with lush meadows, thick forests and fast-running trout streams. The only region of Spain never conquered by the Moors, it was here that the Visigothic kings defended themselves through all those centuries, presumably fortified by a hearty bean stew called *fabada*. The large, flat, white *faba* bean has a unique, delicately buttery flavour and is fine-skinned with creamy, firm flesh. Cooked with air-dried pork shank, streaky bacon and, preferably, oak-smoked *morcilla* blood sausages and *chorizo*, as well as garlic, onions and olive oil, the *fabada* is a robust delight. Alfonso and I tucked into bowls upon juicy bowls of the stuff, mopping it up with bread and washing it all down with hearty red Rioja and further *pacharáns* to follow.

Then it hit me.

I don't know if it was the fact that Alfonso suggested we go on for a *tapas* crawl after work (no doubt still bemused that I was still breathing), or the fact that a whole orchestra had started rehearsals in my belly. Either way, I asked him to stop the taxi near Colón on the way back to the office so that I could 'sort out a few things' in my turquoise *apartamento* and then meet him in 'half an hour or so' to continue with the *tapas* after work. As he grinned at me staggering out of the taxi, I honestly don't think he ever expected to see me again.

With the seismic shuddering in my guts, I took the long way back from the Centro Colón to Sir Rhino Twes, which meant walking straight past the office front door and into the Retiro park, the other side of the Plaza de la Independencia. I would get to love strolling in this beautiful, regal park, particularly on Sunday mornings, but it was also very useful after a heavy Madrid lunch. The statues, manicured flowerbeds and the magnificent tranquil setting of its Palacio de Cristal were so romantic and peaceful that I felt almost guilty in breaking the silence. But needs must, and I spent a pleasant fifteen minutes farting uncontrollably whilst watching the pavement chalk-artists and the rowers on the boating-lake, all the time plucking up courage to join Alfonso for a dose of evening *tapas*.

To *tapear* in Madrid means to go from bar to bar eating small dishes of food – *tapas* – accompanied by several drinks. This is normally done from about eight in the evening, before, but rarely instead of, the later dinner. There are many hundreds of *tapas* bars in Madrid, from Galician bars with octopus and other seafood, to Andalucian bars serving sardines and thin slices of dry-cured tuna loin called *mojama*. There are three basic sizes of *tapa* portions – a *pincho*, which is virtually just a mouthful, a *tapa*, a saucer size, and a *ración*, which is a small plate. Most *tapas* are accompanied by bread – as most Spaniards would rather go without food altogether than eat it without bread. To *tapear* is both a ritual and an art form – knowing what to order, how to catch the barman's attention and how to banter with him while squeezing through for a space at the bar. Personally, I found the whole custom stressful and indigestible – as no sooner had you found space in a bar serving something that tasted delicious, than someone would insist everyone move on elsewhere.

Because of the heavy lunchtime, my first *tapas* experience was not as long and drawn-out as Alfonso would have liked. As we hopped from bar to bar, though, I soon got the hang of it – noting that seats were strictly for tourists, while the locals preferred to stand with a beer or a glass of chilled wine, wolfing back fistfuls of almonds. Most bars displayed the day's *tapas* on a blackboard, and as we nibbled our way through the menu, the barman took a stick of chalk from behind his ear to scrawl down our tab on the bar in front of us, leaving him greying at the temple. A friend of Alfonso's joined us, who spoke no English either, and soon I felt it would be polite to leave them alone together rather than subject them to further sign-language. So after three stops, three *cervezas* and three *tapas*, one of sizzling garlic prawns, one of fried squid rings and one of small fried cuttlefish, I made my excuses to leave, with Alfonso flatly refusing to allow me to pay for anything yet again.

Back in the *apartamento*, despite being alone, I began to feel relieved that nothing else had been arranged for me. I'd be able to discover the city at my own pace over the weekend. It meant spending a long time not talking to anyone, though. So when I *did* finally find someone who understood me, I really went for it.

5

It was my first Friday evening and I was back at the Gijón, doing exactly what Lola, my Spanish teacher in London, had recommended – trying to order a beer at the bar. I'd been there a week and seen others simply shouting, *'Oiga!'* (literally, 'Listen!') and then, *'Caña!'* across many other bars, to be presented shortly afterwards with draught beer. So there was no doubt that *caña* was beer. But when *I* asked for a *caña*, the barman at the Gijón replied with a question.

'*No tenemos caña, solo botellas. Quiere botella?*'

This was rattled off. I didn't understand a word of it.

'Excuse me?' I said.

'He saying they have beer in bottles but not – how you say – *pump*?'

The voice, gentle and sexy, came from a girl standing next to me, and I swear I felt that word 'pump' literally oozing out of her in several syllables, like *'puh-uh-ump'*. She was leaning against the bar with her back to me, and her head twisted round so she could translate what the barman was saying. I nodded politely as the barman uncapped a cold bottle and then I tried to thank her. She twisted her head again, smiled as she met my eye, then stood sideways, which allowed me to get a good look at her. She had jet-black shiny hair, cut short at the back in a French sort of bob. Her fringe dropped forward boyishly over her sparkling, almost oriental eyes. She was quite short – like everyone else, to be honest – but I couldn't take my eyes or mind off her exquisite, classical face. I have to admit that I was immediately obsessed.

Minutes later, two friends joined her, another girl and a young man. They stayed at the bar, ordering more coffee. They carried books and folders like college colleagues. After a while, I asked them if they'd like a drink.

'A drink,' I explained. 'I mean, you know – to thank you – *you*,' I stressed, nodding towards the first girl. 'For helping me order one in the first place.'

The guy, bespectacled and friendly enough, said he had to go, which I assumed meant they all had to go. But the girls looked at one another, then looked at me, and agreed to stay for a beer. But: 'Just the one.'

How lucky do you get?

Not only do two attractive young *Madrileñas* accept your offer of a drink, but then the guy they're with buggers off home as well. Chantal and Cecilia both spoke beautiful, broken English, and wanted to practise it on me as the evening wore on. It was about eight o'clock when they'd said, 'Just the one,' but two in the morning by the time they got me back to my turquoise *apartamento*.

If this was Madrid, then I was staying.

'What-it-is-this that you are doing here?' asked Chantal, the one who'd helped me order the beer. 'Holiday, yes? Or business, yes?'

'Bo-Gay,' I explained, hopelessly transfixed on her sparkling eyes.

'What-it-is-this that is called Bo-Gay?'

'What-it-is-this what?' I whispered to myself. She had a wonderfully erotic voice. 'Bo-Gay,' I explained, 'is a magazine. *Vogue*. You *know*.'

'Ah, *Vogue*. Like *Vogue* Paris?' she said, pronouncing Paris *Parreee*.

'Exactly,' I said. 'Like Vogue *Parreee*. But here they call it Bo-Gay.'

They seemed intrigued. So we had another drink at the Gijón and they suggested another bar. Then another. And another. And I got the feeling that they wanted to show me their city. They were last-year law students – intelligent, trilingual – and they talked a lot about Madrid, its quirkiness and nightlife. They wanted to make sure I knew about not just the old-style Gijón cafés but the flashy music bars too, the ones they believed were 'in vogue' and *should be* in *Vogue*. Shouting at them over the music, I insisted I really wanted to see a more authentic Spain. So they took me to the smoky El Timón.

The *cervecería*, or alehouse, El Timón, was near the Centro Colón itself. El Timón means 'rudder', and the bar's entrance was decorated with a huge ship's steering-wheel and porthole-style windows. Upstairs, it was a normal *tapas* bar, and downstairs, once it was late enough, it became a Sevillana bar. The Sevillana is the dance most often presented to *guiris* like myself as flamenco, and maybe this was a polite effort on the girls' behalf to show me the best they could, and as near to my hotel as possible. But who cares? I thought it was the most sensuous dance in the world, at least by the hour Chantal and Cecilia took me there. The thing that intrigued me most about downstairs at El Timón was that there was no floor-show, just normal couples coming in off the street, simply coming in to drink and dance this entrancing Spanish dance *before* going on somewhere else.

Whilst Chantal and I leant against the bar adorned with light-blue *azulejo* tiles and getting steadily pissed on cold, dry *jerez*, we watched Cecilia dancing with complete strangers – with a huge grin lighting up her face as she looked over at us with wild, excited eyes.

Chantal was actually half-Spanish and half-French. The Café de Gijón, she kept reminding me, had been an appropriate place to have met, because it was where she was born – Gijón – one of the largest cities in Asturias, home of Alfonso's favourite weapon, the *faba* bean. By the time they dropped me off at the Centro Colón, I was legless but deliriously smitten. Cecilia scribbled down their phone numbers for me against their initials, and I managed to focus just enough to make sure I knew which number was Chantal's.

Before arriving in Madrid, I had heard that a new Spanish organisation had recently been formed, called the Federation of Sexology Societies, the 'FESS'.

Its very existence seemed to further underline how Spain had moved on from the repressive days under Franco – when the Catholic Church apparently taught schoolchildren that the penis was the 'diabolical serpent' and the vagina was 'Satan's den'.

The FESS, I'd heard, was going to promote the study of human sexuality throughout Spain, and conduct comprehensive surveys to demonstrate its scientific, educational and therapeutic benefits. I'd also heard that *eighty per cent* of Spaniards already planned the time and location of their sexual encounters. And while sixty-five per cent preferred sex at night, a staggering *thirty-one* per cent of *señoritas* luxuriated in the idea of the diabolical serpent slithering its way into Satan's den during an afternoon *siesta*.

As I stretched out deliriously on the sofa in my turquoise pit at the Colón that night, I did my inebriated maths. Five more weeks in Madrid. Five more weeks before I had to return to my Brixton hell-hole. Five more weeks was thirty-five days. Thirty-five *siestas*. That was a thirty-one per cent chance over thirty-five *siestas* …

6

I woke fully clothed at six with a throbbing hangover on the turquoise sofa, my contact lenses glued to my eyeballs with the tar of black Spanish cigarettes. By eleven, after a brief visit to my bed, I was ready to see Madrid, my first day off in the city.

I set off happily with a map, my pocket dictionary, and the desire to just walk. I hadn't expected it to be raining, but I found a shop in Génova and bought a cheap umbrella. By the time I left the shop, it had stopped raining and the sky was a stunning blue. This was to happen often. Even when it was grey or wet, in Spain you knew that the sun would soon reappear. The Madrid skyline looked beautiful, and the clouds, when they did appear, formed wonderful, flat, pink wisps. It wasn't so much the sun that was stunning, it was the *light*. This light somehow caused in me a strong sense of relief – that things were actually brighter than I'd feared. It was the sky. There's nothing at all like the Madrid sky.

With my naff new umbrella, I tried to stroll along as slowly as all the *Madrileños*, careful not to overtake them all at once. The wet pavements of the Gran Vía glistened in the sunshine as I strolled towards the Plaza de España and sat near the three statues of Cervantes, Don Quixote and Sancho Panza. I watched the people and the honking traffic roll slowly by as I took souvenir photos to remember it by back in London, where the sky presses down on you like the low ceiling of a Brixton basement flat, and to where I'd now already soberly resigned myself returning, despite last night's exhilarating antics.

I didn't have the confidence to try and order Spanish food, so I ended up with a large beer and a spaghetti bolognese in one of the pseudo Swiss-Italian restaurants, full of green and red tablecloths, that seem to serve tourists across Europe. But as I half-heartedly picked at the tasteless rubber pasta plonked in front of me, I missed the local cuisine already. From there, I meandered back up Gran Vía, down Preciados off the Plaza del Callao, and down towards the Puerta del Sol, where one or two cafés had put out tables and chairs on the pavements despite the brisk temperature. I could see windows full of octopus and grotesque-looking fish, and numerous large *tapas* bars like the crazy Ham Museum, el Museu del Jamón, displaying hundreds of hanging pigs' legs.

I went from there to the arcaded Plaza Mayor,

overlooked by balconies that had witnessed executions, coronations, bullfights, the canonizations of saints and the Spanish Inquisition's trials of faith. Many restaurants and bars had also put out chairs and tables, but only the very brave, or the very *loco*, were sitting out at them. I meandered around the twisting alleys and steps adjoining the *plaza* which led me to the majestic Plaza de Oriente and into the Palacio Real where I took a guided tour. This Royal Palace, I learnt, had three thousand rooms, more than any other European palace. I was overwhelmed by its beauty.

Coming out, I could see a cable-car in the distance, making its way across the Casa de Campo, a wide expanse of wooded parkland to the west of Madrid. After a long, exhausting walk, I eventually took the cable-car back over to the city, back towards the Palacio Real across the city's stunning skyline, with the snow-capped peaks of the *sierra* to my left. I felt shattered yet exhilarated. I'd fallen in love with Madrid at every corner of my walk, seduced by the light thrown against the *Madrileño* façades, and the shadows trapped by it under every crevice, arch and balcony. I'd discovered pockets of medieval buildings and narrow, atmospheric alleys, dotted with the oddest shops and bars, and interspersed with eighteenth-century Bourbon squares. It was a beautiful, magnetic city.

That evening, I considered retracing last night's steps in the hope of catching a glimpse of Chantal and Cecilia again, but – still the Englishman – by the time Madrid started coming to life at eleven o'clock, I was back at the *apartamento*, flicking aimlessly through nonsensical TV shows before passing out.

I woke on the turquoise sofa at five in the morning again – and, yes, with my contact lenses firmly married to my eyeballs. A pattern was emerging. By late afternoon, after spending some time in the *apartamento* plotting my plan of attack for the week ahead, I was jogging from Plaza de Colón to the Las Ventas bullring, determined to also tick that off from all the sights my guidebook had recommended. I arrived there, panting and sweating profusely, then collapsed, laying flat on my back on one of the benches, staring up at the ornately designed structure of the arena. It didn't have much impact on me at first, but as I gazed up at it for several minutes, taking in its arabesque style with ceramic designs and decorative pottery, I began to feel a bit odd. It was probably an after-effect of my attempt at exercising a body straining under the recent onslaught of garlic, alcohol and endless feasting, but I suddenly started to feel, well, a bit unusual. As the bullring swirled against the city's pink evening sky, I had this powerful sensation that Madrid would become my home forever.

7

If my first week in Madrid was full of food, the second week was so frantic, there was hardly any time for lunch. Francisco and Alfonso argued amongst themselves until they finally realised there was a good chance *Vogue España* wouldn't be appearing in five weeks. I tried to push things into action but no one understood a bloody word I said.

So I spent my spare time learning parrot-fashion questions to ask everyone in the office. The little Spanish I learned became heavily weighted towards publishing vocabulary. I could soon translate phrases that in any language would leave most native speakers puzzled, such as 'right reading, emulsion side down', but I didn't have a hope in hell of asking to purchase a softer loo-roll in the nearest supermarket.

I bought a portable typewriter from a little shop in the Calle Hortaleza. It was a beautiful old thing, with all the Spanish letters and keys which did upside-down question-marks like ¿, exclamation-marks like ¡ and squashed peseta symbols like **Pts** – as well as the ñ in España. I could really identify with this typewriter. It was my resistance against remaining a sun-burnt *guiri*. If I couldn't learn to pronounce Spanish (and I couldn't), then at least I'd *spell* it correctly. It also meant I could write up my report on *Vogue* Spain, something I was half-way through when, just after a week of being there, I had my first proper meeting with Luis Carta. My report was not encouraging, and I was in two minds how much to tell him. If I'd told him it was all crap or that it was all OK, I could have been on the next flight home. But I wanted to stay.

It was late in the day and getting dark when I was finally summoned by Luis Carta's PA, the matronly shaped and softly spoken María Teresa. Before ushering me into his office, she asked me how my Spanish was coming along. I replied rather flippantly with a simple, '*Mañana*', trying to jokingly imply that I was sure it would start improving from 'tomorrow'.

'*Ma-ñan-a,*' she said, slowly. Then: '*En-yey,*' she stressed, loudly mouthing the letter ñ for me to repeat.

'*En-yey,*' I said, embarrassed.

Then she uttered something that I didn't understand at all, which was, in fact, '*Ñoño Yáñez come ñame en las mañanas con el niño,*' and wrote it down for me to practise. I didn't know what it meant, but it was, she explained, a *'trabalengua'* – a tongue-twister – and it would help me to get that ñ sound just right.

'Try it,' she said. 'Say, "*Ñoño Yáñez come ñame en las mañanas con el niño.*"' Her nose scrunched up as she spoke and the whole thing came out in nasally Spanish. She looked nuts. I took a deep breath and steadied myself.

'*Non yo yan yo com nam man yams –*'

I got no further. María Teresa's cuddly frame crumpled up in giggles. This was to be one of many alphabet pronunciation lessons I was going to have – and the letter ñ was an important one to get right. *Año*, for example, meant 'year', but *ano* meant 'anus'. You had to know what you were doing, therefore, before wishing a Spaniard a happy new year.

'*Gracias*, María Teresa,' I said, pocketing the scrap of paper.

'You're welcome,' she replied, drying her eyes and shooing me in to see *el padrino*.

Luis Carta's office was as cool as he was, and he sat in the dark, apart from a modern, trendy lamp illuminating a tiny corner of the ceiling. His desk wasn't a desk. It was a large, square, marble-top table – almost a boardroom table, with no papers on it at all. He didn't keep any papers, or if he did, you never saw them. If María Teresa put a letter in front of him, he'd read it, scribble his initials on it, and pass it back to her to file. He'd then never refer to it again. He had a photographic memory and could sum up someone just by glancing at them. Whilst there were no papers, he had a glass of water placed on a linen napkin upon his table, as well as a pencil and a writing pad, where he'd list what he wanted to achieve each day. Other than that, there was nothing.

Behind him, black modern shelving held the latest editions of Condé Nast magazines that he currently admired – the Italian and British *Vogues*, as well as *Tatler* and the French décor titles. On the wall was a large, framed, black-and-white photograph of a raunchy blonde shaking her hair as she twisted in a chair, below a lipstick-red *Vogue* logo and the words '*Bravo España*'. I'd pushed open the double sliding-doors to present myself, and Luis, with that very faint *Godfather* wave using just his closed fingers, beckoned me to come further inside.

'*Teeeeem*,' he said (and no one said *Teeeeem* with as many *e*s as Luis). 'Come. Let's talk. *Venga, hablamos*,' he said. 'Tell me things. Tell me.'

He kept saying, 'Tell me'. It was a literal translation of *digame* in Spanish. I think deep down Luis was quite an anglophile. His Italian suits had that hint of Englishness about them, and there was always a dash of something eccentric in his style – undone cuffs and collars on the unbuttoned-down shirt, bright socks, a red handkerchief or even his Rolex watch clipped firmly *on top of* his shirt cuffs. He had a big, round, tanned face and high receding forehead, and spoke to me partly in English to practise it, partly in Spanish, and partly in what sounded like Italian. But he spoke so slowly that I understood every single word.

'Luis,' I said, taking a seat and spreading some of my papers across the marble desk. 'I've got something that I've started to prepare ...'

He waved his *Godfather* hand with a simple 'I already know. *Ya lo sé.*'

'Look,' I said, insisting a little. 'I've only been here a week but there are things I've already noticed and so I've started to write it all up in this report that I'm –'

'Tell me,' he said, doing the beckoning thing with his fingers again.

I told him we weren't on schedule.

'Don't tell me any more. I know. I already know.'

I wondered what this meant. If he already knew, why was I there?

'That's why you're here,' he said.

'I'm sorry?'

'I knew – I told Francisco – that we should invite you here to guide us. We would have been mad not to. He told you I said this, yes?'

'Yes, yes, *but* –' I started.

'Let me show you,' interrupted Luis, suddenly standing up and walking around the marble-top table to my side. 'Come,' he said, tapping me on the shoulder.

I stood up and joined him. He guided me around his office a little, then pushed the sliding-doors open and started to guide me around the reception area, too, past María Teresa, whilst pointing up at the walls, ceilings, fixtures and fittings.

'Look!' he exclaimed, indicating some bad paintwork above the bookshelves near Giovanni's table. 'They never finished it! I asked María Teresa to tell them to come back in, but *nada* – nothing – *nada!*' Luis strung *'nada'* out into a high-pitched whine of *'Naaaadaaaa!'* He went on: 'They never came back! They don't know how to finish anything properly in this country. *Naaaaaadaaaaaa!* This is why you're here.' He pointed out the bad finishing and paintwork. I wondered if he wanted me to get out a brush. 'We know that it's bad timing – bad finishing, half-completing everything – and we want you to help. Now, one thing is to know this problem that we have,' he added, as we edged our way back towards his office. 'Another thing is to solve it. Are you able to put it right?'

'I believe I can,' I said. 'If I can just get people to understand me.'

There were often pauses between Luis's sentences, and once we were back in his office, he rubbed his chin thoughtfully.

'I like you,' he said, as simply as that. 'But you'll have to work. We all have to work. You do *want* to work here, yes?'

I nodded.

'Maybe there's something here for you. But you'll have to work.'

'I can work.'

'For now, you have to force them to work faster and to your system, because we have to get this first issue out …' There was a pause. 'Then we'll talk.' There was another pause. 'Then we'll talk some more.' He pushed my papers back across the table, my cue to leave.

'When do you go back to London?' he asked.

'Well, I'm here for another four weeks –'

'We'll talk again a week before you leave.' There was another pause. He scribbled a note to remind himself. 'Why Spain?' he asked, not looking up.

'I'm sorry?'

'Why do you want to live in Spain?'

I looked at him for a moment. OK, it wasn't the whitewashed, bougainvillaeaed, olive-grove Spain of North European fantasies. But I suddenly thought about the sky over Madrid and that special *light*. I thought about all the glorious food, the Rioja wine and Chantal's almond eyes. I thought about the taste of *pacharán*, the cool tumblers of *cerveza* and delicious *tapas* in the magnificent Espejo bar. And I thought about my ball-breaking on-off 'ex' back in England who kept phoning the turquoise *apartamento* to suggest reigniting our torrid relationship. I'd kept telling her it was over, but the calls kept coming. So I answered Luis as honestly as I could.

'I like it here,' I said.

Still pinching myself that I was even in Madrid at all, I started to dwell on the potential of a real future. I caused further chaos in the office, visited the repro house with the loud Mayte to interpret, then rewrote all the schedules to show how things should be done. This upset Alfonso, but we agreed to disagree and, because we still didn't understand a word one another said, we couldn't really *argue* about it.

Luis wanted a cover image for the poster and TV campaign, and, having scurried around for days, Francisco came up with something which, by coincidence, was in line with José Manuel's promotional gifts: a Latin-looking Cindy Crawford holding a red fan, *à la española*, with her dark hair, her beauty spot, her blood-red lipstick, her red *abanico*, all complementing the red *Vogue España* logo.

We worked late one night preparing a dummy issue for José Manuel's posters. Then, the next morning, Ramón, the rather scary-looking, scarred advertising manager, casually let slip that he'd sold a gatefold cover to Estée Lauder 'weeks ago'. A gatefold cover is one of those fold-out jobs where the advertiser takes a 'treble-page-spread' at the front of the magazine, and editorial is left with a front cover that folds out to display a double page of a *horizontal* model, or whatever the hell it likes, anything other than just a portrait shot of Cindy Crawford on her own.

'So, what's going on the page that folds out?' I asked Francisco.

'What page that folds out?'

At that moment, I lost it. I grabbed Francisco, Alfonso, Ana and José Manuel, pushed them all into Luis's office, and ranted and raved in English. We'd spent *days* trying to get the sodding cover right! If we'd known about the gatefold, we could have designed the cover to accommodate it and sold the extra flap to Estée bloody Lauder! Were we even *crediting* Cindy Crawford's make-up as Estée Lauder? And if we *were*, we could have got them to sponsor the red fans, too – and then had the fan opening up on to the page that folds out and used it for the *poxy fucking poster campaign*!

When I'd finished, there was a hideous, stunned silence. I assumed I'd be on the next flight home.

'What did he say?' asked Alfonso.

8

Chantal met me at the Gijón at nine. She looked radiant and I immediately got a kick out of the fact that we were meeting alone, without Cecilia, as if already on some illicit secret affair. I'd called her a few days earlier from my lonely, rancid *apartamento*, and when she arrived, she reminded me about the slurred call.

'So, what-it-is-this you said you wanted to do?' she purred, teasing me with her come-to-bed accent. 'You say you want to see every bar, yes? Is this, yes?'

'Yes,' I gulped, polishing off my bottle of *cerveza*. 'Is this.'

Oh, yes, *is this*.

We grabbed a taxi and she directed it down Recoletos, past Cibeles and towards the floodlit fountains surrounding Neptune in the Plaza de Cánovas del Castillo, where the exclusive Hotel Ritz looked across to the equally glitzy Hotel Palace, then up San Jerónimo, where Chantal pointed out Las Cortes, the Parliament building guarded by two large bronze lions. She took me to the core of this throbbing district, to the Plaza de Santa Ana, explaining the former glory of the bullfighters' hangout, the Hotel Reina Victoria, before we dived into the nearby Cervecería Alemana. We strolled on from bar to bar, talking, drinking, getting to know one another, taking in the wall-to-wall tiled hangouts of Los Gabrieles and then Viva Madrid, complete with its original zinc bar. As we edged our way through the throng, she slipped her arm through mine, gently squeezing it. I tried to thank her for showing me what I assumed was a *guiri's* Madrid, but she insisted it wasn't just a tourist area. As the fun rolled on and I witnessed more and more *Madrileños* enjoying this heaving Thursday night, I realised she was right. This was how the Spanish lived.

Chantal explained that this was called *marcha* – going out to drink and dance until the early hours, often through the night, a consequence and continuation of the *movida Madrileña*, the 'Madrid scene', the early-eighties explosion of liberated creativity among Madrid's youth. Going out until the early hours and getting slowly wrecked was something that I was going to have to get used to. But having been drinking since six-thirty at the turquoise *apartamento* for Dutch courage before I'd met her, I hadn't a hope in hell of pacing myself at all. Instead, I was slaughtered by midnight, when, according to the rules of a *marcha*, we still had at least three hours to go.

'So, how is your Spanish coming on, yes?' Chantal joked much later, knowing damn well that I was no better at ordering *cañas* than on the first night we'd met.

'*Non yo yan yo com nam man yams,*' I dribbled, unfolding the scrap of paper that María Teresa had given me. Chantal quickly snatched it.

'*Ñoño Yáñez come ñame?*' she cried.

'S'posed to puh-ractise it,' I slurred. 'Wotsit mean?'

'It means ... well, it means that Ñoño Yáñez – a man – eats ... how you say this? Yams? Yes, yams is sweet potato, yes? Yes, is this: "Ñoño Yáñez eats yams in the morning with the boy."'

'Non Yon Yan Yon?' By that point I couldn't even say it in English.

I wanted to see Chantal again but I was in no fit state to ask her up for a nightcap and demonstrate how my porter had shown me how to ski in the turquoise *apartamento* – no, not yet. So I didn't know what the next step might be, but she was very cool, determined, clever, irresistible.

'So, when-it-is-this that we do this again, yes?' she said.

After another fitful sleep, I was picked up just four hours later by Alfonso and his daughter, Eva, who was ten years old but spoke perfect English. On the roof of Alfonso's car were two sets of skis. They were going skiing in Navacerrada, an hour and a bit from Madrid, and had invited me along for the scenic ride.

I strolled and sat at a terrace café in the sun, taking in the fresh mountain air whilst they skied. Probably conscious that I'd been left alone, Alfonso and Eva rejoined me an hour or so later, suggesting we head via Segovia to a place called Pedraza for lunch. We took the long, winding, pine-fringed road down the mountain towards Segovia, taking a small detour past the imposing Roman Aqueduct in the Plaza de Azoguejo, while Eva translated Alfonso's explanations of how it once carried water from the river *Eresma*.

Leaving Segovia with its cobblestone-squares and honey-coloured stone monuments, we headed north along the Soria road towards Pedraza, with Alfonso pointing out the occasional abandoned Castilian fortress en route. It was a stunning journey, and Pedraza itself, once we finally arrived, was magical, with an intoxicating smell of wood-burning fires spiced with the aroma of cooking, as restaurants prepared for lunchtime visitors.

We drove slowly through the original gateway entrance to the village from where the narrow lanes spiralled gently up towards the *plaza mayor*. Here, we stopped for a lunch of succulent lamb, roasted Castilian-style in a wood oven, washing it all down with a jug of red house wine, and mopping it up with chunks of bread and salad, dripping in olive oil. This was more like it. I felt relaxed and even snug – almost in sunburnt holiday mood, flushed and glowing from the mountain sun and air – and I wanted Eva to translate something back to her father. I told her to explain that I was sorry if I'd been 'getting in his way' in the office, and she spoke rapidly with him for several minutes before she beamed happily back at me.

'He says he's also sorry if he's, how you say – getting in *your* way.'

We left it like that, toasting one another with ice-cold *pacharáns*.

9

'I read your report,' said Luis Carta, once I'd finally been called back into his office. There followed one of his long pauses. 'You leave here when?' he finally added, thoughtfully stroking his chin again.

'In a week,' I said. 'A week this Sunday is when I actually fly.'

'OK, this is what I want you to do …'

The consequences of what he said next meant there was no need for me to check out of my *apartamento*.

'Just take a couple of shirts back to England,' he said. 'You have to tell them I need you for another three months. You should spend about a week in London to sort things out, then come back. I need you here. I'll tell Daniel, the chairman, but you have to tell Condé Nast London. They'll let you come back. They'll understand …'

He said 'they'll understand' with another one of his

Godfather flicks of the hand, dismissing them in one tiny gesture, as if to say, if they didn't understand, he'd cut the heads off a few racehorses and plant them under their duvets. This was Luis in a nutshell, asking me to arrange my own future. There was no formal letter to carry back to England, no 'memo' from Condé Nast Spain to Condé Nast London. Nothing at all, apart from his 'word'.

After our conversation, I propped up the bar at the Espejo en route back to the Colón. I had fallen in love with this place – its decorative tiled walls of half-clad mermaids, the huge mirrors with the Art Deco curved corners, the dark wood, the chessboard tiled floor, the big brass beer pump in the middle of the central bar with the proud eagle on top, the red velvet creaky chairs, and in the middle of it all, a huge chandelier of crystal white rose bulbs. It looked older than it apparently was, but I didn't care – there was no better place to sip cold *cervezas* and eat *pinchos* of *tortilla* and canapés of *cangrejo* crab.

The beer tasted like ambrosial nectar and I just stood there, mumbling madly at the mirrored walls whilst raising a glass to myself. I felt intoxicated with relief, as though I'd just been granted a reprieve from a life sentence in grim, grey London. Because I was alone, I forced myself to chat (in what I believed to be Spanish) with the cross-eyed barman who always appeared to be looking over my shoulder as he listened to me. Or maybe he *was* looking over my shoulder, trying to ignore me.

Back in London it took them thirteen days to 'understand'. When I returned to Madrid's Barajas airport, I was immediately struck by the smoke. Madrid airport had the only arrival lounge I knew of where you could still light up while waiting for your luggage to roll through. Smoking in Spain is epidemic.

Everyone was happy with the first issue of *Vogue España* – which finally came out because Alfonso had surrendered to my schedule – and which was selling well, thanks mainly to the TV and poster campaigns, and because launch editions normally do sell well.

I threw myself back into the job with a vengeance, combining my lunchtimes and evenings taking Spanish lessons with my new teacher, the freckly, funky Beatriz. Alfonso and I battled to try and get the May issue out on time, but things just weren't going smoothly.

The first hint that something was going on behind the scenes was when Ildefonso, the short, squat, balding *director financiero*, suddenly started being nice to me – and then even more bizarrely, asked me for lunch. Now, lunch with a finance director was always going to be a much more sober affair than lunch with, say, Alfonso or Francisco. A finance director, especially the tight-fisted Ildefonso, needed to observe frugality and modesty. He needed to observe that I didn't drink, at least not heavily, and that I didn't order the most expensive starter or over-binge on the main course, even if he did, because finance directors rarely get invited out. It would go down well with a finance director if I could manage to drink only mineral water, even if he didn't, definitely pass on the offer of desserts, cigars or after-lunch *pacharán*, and even offer half-heartedly to pay. It was going to be a long lunch for all the wrong reasons.

I did everything that was expected of me. I ate and drank frugally, agreed with his politics and outlook on life, and answered his poorly disguised final question of whether or not ... I mean, *just supposing* ... it would be possible for me to *not* finally return to England at the end of June.

'Well ... Ildefonso,' I felt like replying. 'It'll mean I won't be able to return to my burgled, fungus-ridden armpit of a flat in Brixton, or face the possibility of seeing my psychotic on-off 'ex' again, which is going to be hard to swallow. Secondly, of course, the licensing laws are sensibly still restricted in England – and a jolly good thing, too, don't you think? – so it's going to be an absolute bloody nightmare staying on permanently in a city where I can always get a drink after eleven at night. And *if* I stay, I'm going to have to see some bullfights and stalk more ravishing *Madrileñas*, see more of the exotic Chantal and her group of friends, and stuff my face with exquisite chilled *jerez* in the sublime surroundings of the Plaza de Santa Ana, then spend more happy hours farting helplessly in Madrid's sun-kissed parks, too, and *that'll* soon take its toll. But other than that, mate, *no problemo!* Fancy another *Perrier*? Here, let me pay for all this.'

But instead, I said, 'Well, I'd be willing to stay on, I suppose … just as long as Condé Nast make it worth my while.'

And so they doubled my salary.

I'd had two and half months with Alfonso, arguing in sign-language and getting away with things because it still wasn't my responsibility if it all went arse over tit. But once they asked him to leave, I realised that things were really getting quite serious.

Luis called me in to confirm that Alfonso had other job offers he was pursuing and that he'd been compensated financially. So it was official, he said – I'd got the job. Ildefonso, the finance director, took great delight in being the one to finalise all the minor details, which consisted of a maximum of three more months, all expenses paid, in the turquoise *apartamento* before I would need to find my own flat to rent. He said they'd also pay for the removal to Spain of any furniture and belongings from the Brixton hell-hole, *and* pay the deposit on any flat I eventually did find.

'And we'll also pay for your Spanish lessons …' he concluded.

Not that it helped.

Alfonso and I went for a final lunch. We still talked in sign language, but he seemed OK about everything. We kept in touch afterwards and often met for a drink. And while I was secretly chuffed that I'd finally landed a role as a real '*Jefe*', I was starting to wonder how I would be able to manage myself when all I really now craved was more *Madrileño marcha*.

10

The Spain to which I'd arrived in 1988 was enjoying only its second decade of democracy. It was a Spain still awash in freedom after a long night of autocratic rule, enjoying 'a renaissance of cultured spirit'. It was a Spain in hyper-development with a five per cent yearly growth rate that far outstripped that of the rest of Europe. Still torn between its old and new image, the country was snowballing from its *movida* years towards its 1992 orgy, which would see the Barcelona Olympics, the Expo in Seville, and Madrid as the Cultural Capital of Europe. Intent on avoiding the rest of Europe's recession, the PSOE, the Partido Socialista Obrero Español (Spanish Socialist Workers Party), was in power and the then popular Felipe González, Prime Minister. His increasing confrontations with the pot-bellied leader of the unions, however, were to culminate in a general strike later in the year, while the ugly, very public battle for supremacy between the country's two major banks, Banesto and Banco Central, epitomised the prevailing mood as the culture of the yuppies (or 'you-pees' as they pronounced it) sought to transplant 'old Spain'.

The gossip magazines were full not of soap-star showbiz news but of entrepreneur socialites such as the two 'Albertos' – Alberto Alcocer and Alberto Cortina – cousins and brothers-in-law, and two 'you-pee' icons always dressed in identical detective-style raincoats. Their messy separations from their lush, marchioness wives, the mega-wealthy sisters, Esther and Alicia Koplowitz, took up acres upon acres of newsprint, especially after *Interviú* magazine published a centre-fold-spread of Cortina's girlfriend, Marta Chávarri (herself the daughter of the government's Chief of Protocol), wearing nothing but tights under her miniskirt in a nightclub. *Interviú* had to reprint several times to meet the overwhelming demand, all because poor Marta had worn *nothing but tights*. The level of interest and shock surrounding these photos seemed absurd, and yet the combination of hedonism, sex, scandal, politics and money all perfectly captured the *Madrileño* zeitgeist.

Hedonism seemed to be inviting itself into my own social life, too – although unfortunately not with any gratifying results. In fact, my diabolical serpent was getting pretty restless, if you must know. I was still in touch with Chantal, but she seemed to always be in the middle of Spanish law exams and not often around.

I'd been busy exploring, too, venturing out on my

own, and I soon realised that the *Madrileños* really did survive on a minimum of sleep. I'd been touring as many smoky bars, *bodegas*, *tabernas* and *cervecerías* as I could find – most of them in the old quarter and near the Plaza de Santa Ana, mapped out with old recommendations from Alfonso, as well as venues I'd been legless in with Chantal and Cecilia. Everywhere I went was packed, both inside and out on the streets, where potent groups of kids swigged from party-size beer bottles – with lots of snogging and loud, loose talk, and always a strong whiff of cannabis smoke in the air.

Because I still couldn't speak any coherent Spanish, I'd end up performing tip-toeing masquerades behind the crowds at each bar, too insecure to shout for exactly what I wanted – and only able to point directly at my wish-list of *tapas* once I'd elbowed my way through the throng. Unlike at my friendly local, the Espejo, most of the staff at these nicotine-tiled dives worked like maniacs, rudely shouting and skidding along the floor behind the bar, mocking customers and hurling plates of food at them. When I hesitated over my order for a nano-second, one swarthy, thick-lipped barman walked off with his eyes raised to the ceiling in exasperation. I didn't know what to do: 'Go back to your turquoise *apartamento* and cut your losses, you sad git!' or 'Hang on in there, fatty … another Chantal-lookalike might yet arrive and help you order the right thing!' And sure enough, more sylph-like, dusky *Madrileñas* would slowly saunter in, wearing tight, taut, short, racy leather skirts, and my diabolical serpent would stay adamantly glued to the bar.

No-one ever talked to me, though.

In fact I soon began to fear that meeting Chantal had all been just a fluky one-off. After fighting through to the counter at one bar, I decided to stand there holding *two* drinks. One, because it had taken so long to get served in the first place, and two, because I thought I'd look cool and approachable if I pretended to be already waiting for someone, which, in a sense, I suppose I was. I thought if I hogged an extra bar stool, *someone* would have to talk to me before dawn. But they didn't. Instead, I looked increasingly suspicious. Whoever I was waiting for was either having a major crap-attack in the loo, or had firmly stood me up.

As I downed more and more *cervezas* on my own, it was clear that *I* was the one who needed to start a conversation. I didn't want to fart around. I wanted to dive straight in. Somewhat woozily, I thought of a good chat-up line: 'I can remove the spider from your bath!' It seemed to me, at that moment, to conjure up images of someone brave, clever, kind and sexy. But I didn't have a clue what *spider* was in Spanish. Which was really my major problem … I couldn't speak!

It dawned on me that the only reason Chantal had ever spoken to me in the first place, was because I *couldn't* speak Spanish properly …

As I waved at the barman to refill my glass again, my boozy thoughts turned to matters in my immediate vicinity, when I sensed that an attractive woman was already standing very close to me and pawing my arm. She was with her boyfriend, it seemed, but it was a start.

'You have fire?' she said.

'Fire?' I thought. Yes, I had fire. In fact I was already in fucking flames.

'Fire, yes?' she said, holding up her cigarette.

She wanted a light!

And she could tell I was a complete and utter *guiri*.

She hadn't even tried to talk to me in her native tongue. I shook my head, apologetic that I was unable to ignite her fire, and I spent the rest of the evening mumbling to a saucer of almonds on the bar.

The next night I met Isabelle. Well, I actually met Daniel, Judith *and* Isabelle. It was a Friday and I'd walked into another one of the bars that Chantal had once taken me to, and I overheard Daniel, an American banker living in Madrid, and Judith, a young, rather hairy Mexican lawyer, and Isabelle, an even younger, blonde Swedish model with flawless, creamy skin, all talking to one another in English, and I just thought I'd join in as quickly as possible.

They asked me what I was doing in Madrid. I said I was working for Bo-Gay (which I now realised was a good opening line), and so they took me to the yuppie venue of the Café Castellana, or 'No.8' in the Castellana for those in the know, and then on to the Archy nightclub, where we jumped all the queues because

Isabelle was obviously one of the resident models or something, kissing everyone from the barmen to the bouncers and DJs, the lot. But then she kept dancing up towards me while I was trying to perch invisibly somewhere, avoiding having to dance. I was, however, totally transfixed by her alarmingly blue eyes as she gyrated and pouted slowly beside me. She was gorgeous.

Yes, Isabelle was leggy, svelte, stunning and very young. For a while, after that evening, she kept turning up uninvited at the Sir Rhino Twes offices to 'collect me' after work. But my on-off attempts at getting her into the turquoise *apartamento* were initially hindered by my involvement with Chantal and my suspicion that she was really just trying to get into Spanish *Vogue*, rather than actually wanting to be with someone like me. If that was her plan, it nearly worked …

Isabelle had arrived one day at reception as Luis sauntered past. She was wearing this wide-brimmed light-blue hat which matched her incredible eyes. Sure enough, I wasn't the only one for a soft spot for blondes.

'*Teeeeeem,*' Luis said to me a few days later, mischievously beckoning me into his office. 'Your girl-friend … the blonde one. Tell me. *Tell me.* The one who keeps picking you up after work. She's very beautiful. *Es muy guapa.*'

'Sure,' I said. 'She's *muy guapa*. But she's not my –'

'*Muy, muy guapa,*' he insisted.

We stared at one another, both smiling, and left it like that. But a week later, our new multi-lingual fashion director, Lisa Lovatt-Smith, called to say that she needed to speak to me. We met in a secluded office down the corridor.

'Luis tells me you have a fabulous girlfriend who's blonde,' she said.

'Well, I wouldn't say she's really my girlfriend –' I started.

'Do you have her number? Luis wants us to photograph her for the cover. He's fed up with Spanish brunettes and wants a blonde.'

'Are you serious?'

Yes, she was.

So I phoned Isabelle. She had a cold which meant she had a red nose, but she was flattered to be asked. She went to the studio to do the shoot, but looked tired, so the photos didn't come out well. This was either an indication of how limited Condé Nast Spain's budgets were, or how half-arsed their planning was. I mean, if a so-called girlfriend of mine could be tested for the cover just because Luis fancied her, then surely something was badly wrong.

Meanwhile, Isabelle and I continued to fail to get it together. There was something about her that I just couldn't handle. Then one evening, everything became clear. She'd invited herself back to the *apartamento*. We'd drunk a lot. It was getting very late and she invited herself to stay over, neatly and bizarrely unpacking a tiny, prearranged overnight bag which I hadn't even noticed her bring in. She started to dance and flirt in front of me, moving slowly over to my cheap cassette player on the floor, and then exaggeratedly bending over as low as she possibly could to change the music on it, while keeping her long legs straight. With her back still turned towards me, she slowly, provocatively edged her skirt up her legs, the type of thing that really taunts you and turns you on and remains tortuously embedded in your mind forever. She came over to me, and her mouth tasted of sweet strawberry lipsalve. We drank some more and she started to undress, telling me that she was excited about the idea of not being a virgin.

And I burst out laughing.

After the nights I'd spent with her on and off, seeing her flirt in Archy and all the other nightclubs and terrace bars around Madrid, seeing all those *Madrileños* swooning over her, all as confused as me, it finally clicked. 'Sod it,' I thought, coming over all English. I mean, I *couldn't*, could I? Not with Chantal in the background and my life confusing enough as it was. I didn't even know her age.

We didn't see much more of one another after that.

I know I'm mad.

I *know*.

11

Meeting Luis and getting to grips with *Vogue España* paralleled my attempts to understand Spain itself. He often came out with statements such as, 'The biggest problem in Spain is the excess of oil in the food,' and he would then explain that such excess was typical of the Spanish problem of extreme, excessive or exaggerated behaviour. In Madrid, nothing was ever done half-heartedly. I was often introduced as *the* most kind, *the* most intelligent or *the* most this or that by Spanish colleagues who hardly knew me at all. From the late hour of doing things, to the feverish football supporting, to over-eating, expressing emotions, even an instance of dressing kids in tiny sailor outfits for first communions – *everything* in Spain seemed a bit over the top.

A fashion picture, for example, could never simply be 'OK'. It was either *una mierda* (a piece of shit) or *de puta madre*, implying the dog's bollocks, the most amazing photo in the universe, *ever.* In Spain, there was simply no room for anything that might possibly fall between the piece of shit and the dog's bollocks.

And then there was always too much of that back-slapping going on, too. I quickly got used to watching otherwise perfectly normal Spanish businessmen constantly slapping the crap out of one another. It never ceased to shock me that whenever I met one for the first time, I'd then be over-complimented on something I hadn't even done, or didn't even own. All this *'íntimo amigo mío'* stuff was bizarre, too. It meant 'my intimate friend', but where the hell did *that* all come from? Was that really how the country worked? I mean, often not a business lunch, not even a coffee, not even an innocent exchange of business-cards had ever taken place, yet Spanish businessmen still had this habit of claiming someone whom they'd never properly met (and always someone more important than themselves) to be an *'íntimo, íntimo amigo mío'*. It was mostly a load of bull.

And whilst I still couldn't pronounce Spanish, my understanding of the language was improving enough to gather what they were saying with *'Yo voy a ser muy sincero'* – 'I'm going to be very sincere' – or *'Yo sólo digo la verdad'* – 'I only ever tell the truth'. I heard them all the time on those TV *'tertulia'* debates, prefixing whatever they were about to say with 'I'm going to tell you the truth.' Well, thanks a lot! You'd hardly start with 'I'm just about to talk a load of fucking bollocks', would you? I mean, who the hell would vote for you?

But the one that really aggravated me was '*Mi casa es tuya*', meaning, 'My house is yours'. Who were they trying to kid? The Spanish very rarely entertained at home – it was always in bars, restaurants or hotels – and so the offer of '*Mi casa es tuya*' was not only confusing but a complete con. It was often uttered to me after meeting someone for the very first time, after I'd innocently mentioned that I might be planning to visit their area of Madrid or elsewhere in Spain. I suppose it could have just meant, 'call in', but then why didn't they simply *say* 'call in'? Instead, it was, 'Well, then, my dear Timothy. My house is yours!' And more: '*Todo lo que tú quieras!*' 'Everything you want!' In other words, they'd spent twenty years or so working their socks off to buy their own house and all its contents – and they'd met me for just a few minutes, but I could now have it all, every single thing. But if I even dared to turn up on their doorstep to say, 'Hi!', let alone 'Er, you jolly well said this house is mine' – well, in Spain, they wouldn't be in.

The Spanish didn't like to finish anything, either, as though any kind of closure was to be mistrusted. I mean, take the simple act of saying goodbye or *adiós*. Easy enough, no? Well, *no*, actually, not for your average Spaniard. In fact it was never just *adiós* at all. It was *adiós* to the power of three. You can see this at any Spanish airport, where entire Spanish families turn up and get in each other's way just to see off a bemused member of the family who's trying to escape for the weekend. They all take it in turns to sob on the embarrassed traveller's shoulders – '*adiós, adiós, adiós*' – blowing kisses, then wailing and waving at them even while they're getting frisked by the baggage-control inspectors. '*Adiós, adiós, adios!*'

I hated this Spanish trait most whenever a group of us left a restaurant after a three-hour lunch or dinner. How much more time together did they *need?* I'd be standing on the pavement, half-pissed and bloated, dying to get into a taxi and head home, when all of a sudden, after numerous kisses on both cheeks and a thousand *adióses*, someone would say, 'Oh, I forgot to tell you …' and we'd all end up standing outside for another half-an-hour. I lost count of the number of *taxistas* I'd wave down only to let them drive off again. 'If you can't say goodbye, let's go back inside the sodding restaurant!' I'd want to shout.

It's true, though: all 'final decisions' and 'closures' were extremely rare in Spain. I'd endlessly read reports in the newspapers of high-profile crooks being sentenced to twenty years or so in prison for major fraud, but then a minute later, it was never absolutely certain that they'd be jailed at all. If you really wanted to make money in Spain, there was at least one simple way: become an Appeal Judge.

The best example of Spanish excess, however, had to be the number of national holidays. There was 1 January, of course, and then the 6th, too, which was Epiphany, then 19 March, good old San José, then a couple of days over Easter, the Jueves and Viernes Santos, and then 1 May, Labour Day; but then somehow they managed to slip in a few more on 15 August (Assumption Day), 12 October (Fiesta Nacional), 1 November (All Saints), as well as two days very close to each other on 6 December (Constitution Day) and 8 December (Immaculate Conception). So that was already eleven, excluding Christmas Day. But then not only were there national holidays but many regional ones, too, with towns and cities all over Spain enjoying several of their own *fiestas* and 'saint's days'.

The only way I ever knew we were on the eve of some *fiesta*, however, was when the matronly María Teresa came in with a new bouffant, beehive hairdo and some kind of ceremonial bouquet-brooch of moss and twigs pinned to her mono-bosom. Special marzipan-flavoured treats and tempting truffles also started to appear on her desk for us all to sample – traditional *Madrileño* cakes, pastries or sweets to commemorate whatever we were supposed to commemorate.

It was thanks to María Teresa that I soon discovered that even Spanish proverbs were overblown. Whilst for the English, for example, a bird in the hand is worth just two in the bush, Spaniards would think it far better to have one in the hand than *hundreds* flying. I discovered all these because she kept bombarding me with them to accompany each special occasion, while feeding me with no end of Spanish *trabalenguas*. This was all very kind, but it meant I was to spend a lot of time muttering rubbish such as, *'Pepe Peña pela papa, pica piña, pita un pito, pica piña, pela papa, Pepe Peña,'* which meant, 'Pepe Peña peels potatoes, cuts a pineapple, blows a whistle, cuts a pineapple (again), peels potatoes (again), does Pepe Peña.' Now, the fact that I could get my tongue around all that was absolutely terrific, according to María Teresa (who was very proud of me), but totally bloody useless when I should have been discussing the cost of our printing. Not only that, but the rest of the staff must have assumed I was a schizo. When colleagues asked me how my weekend was, I'd be likely to froth that I'd hung out with Barry, a big black-backed busy bumble-bee in a brown balaclava, or even with Catalina, a climbing caterpillar who had three baby caterpillars and when the climbing caterpillar climbed, the three baby caterpillars climbed as well. '*Una cacatrepa trepa tiene tres cacatrepitos, cuando la cacatrepa trepa trepan los tres cacatrepitos!*' I'd spray. Their voices said, 'That's *fantastico, Teeeem,*' but their eyes said, 'Where's the strait-jacket?'

María Teresa was extremely sweet and very generous with all her softly-spoken explanations of Spanish customs and folklore, but I was literally getting very hot and bothered with one particular rhyming phrase that she kept repeating to me: '*Hasta el cuarenta de Mayo, no te quites el sayo*'. *Sayo* meant 'tunic', and so María Teresa was really telling me that I shouldn't take my tunic off until 40 May. There were actually only thirty one days in May – even in Spain – and I didn't even own a fucking tunic. What she was trying to warn me about was the Madrid weather: deceivingly warm during the daylight but frequently cold enough at night to freeze the *cojones* off the bravest bull. There was an old *Madrileño* proverb that said the city's icy wind would fail to extinguish a nun's candle but could snuff out any Spaniard, whatever the size of his serpent. So by keeping my tunic buttoned up until 40 May really meant I should keep a jacket on until 9 June. I appreciated the advice, but it was bloody hot out there. For a poor *guiri* like me, this was the height of sodding summer. What was María Teresa on about? Where had Luis found her? I spent days sweltering whilst waiting for 9 June, anxious to not take my jacket off in case I was seen by María Teresa in my shirt-sleeves, and then have her pounce on me or force some commemorative marzipan down my throat. When she did see me, she always had another rhyming phrase to throw at me, too. It was, '*Timoteo, que te veo!*' which rhymed beautifully in Spanish, but simply meant, 'I see *yooooooou*, Timothy!' Harmless enough ... if I'd been her five-year-old grandchild.

I obviously had lots to learn, though, when it came to the Madrid heat. The word I'd found for 'hot' was *caliente*, so when I told María Teresa that, '*Estoy caliente,*' I'd merely assumed I was saying, 'I'm hot.'

But I wasn't.

'*Caliente,*' Francisco explained to me, also meant 'randy'. To tell María Teresa that I was bloody baking with my so-called tunic on, I should have instead been saying, '*Tengo calor*' – 'I have heat' – in the Latin way.

What I'd actually been saying was something like 'I'm feeling so randy, María Teresa, so hot and horny for you, my sexy baby.' I must have sounded like Barry

White. No wonder she kept telling me to keep my tunic buttoned up.

Despite her sweet-natured efforts of swamping me with all her knowledge of traditional Spanish etiquette, María Teresa also failed to explain anything at all to me about *puentes* – 'bridges'. You see, in addition to all those national and regional holidays that existed in Spain, one had to also take into account the *puentes*. Your average *puente* worked very simply. In England, a bank holiday was always arranged to fall on a Monday regardless of its official date. Such a thing was unheard of in Spain. 1 May was 1 May, and if it fell on a Tuesday or a Thursday, the holiday remained on that Tuesday or Thursday. That's where the crafty old *puente* came in – because the Spanish, the clever buggers, had this wonderful habit of 'bridging' their weekends across to any midweek holiday by taking off the Monday or Friday, too.

Now, that was all very well until you arrived at those two dates in the first week of December, when Spaniards happily celebrated their Constitution swiftly followed by an Immaculate Conception. But what happened when the Constitution fell on a Tuesday and the Immaculate Conception a Thursday? Did they take two *puentes*, going to work only on the Wednesday?

Cojones, did they.

'Where *is* everyone?' I asked María Teresa on the first week of December, when I turned up at the office and saw no one there at all other than her, the week we were supposed to be sending the January edition off to the printers.

'Oh, they're all doing the *viaducto*,' she said. 'Do you want some marzipan?'

'The what?'

'Marzipan –'

'The via-*what*?'

'The *viaducto*,' she said. 'The viaduct. It's when they take the Monday, Wednesday and Friday off … as well as the Tuesday and Thursday. Would you like some pre-Christmas *roscón* cake?'

María Teresa's '*roscón*' cake, it turned out, was actually '*El Roscón de Reyes*', which, legend has it, the Three Kings used to leave at the homes of the poor and destitute as they passed through town, no doubt en route for their own long *viaducto* vacation.

'Woscon de weyes?' I said, and the poor old girl nearly choked.

12

Madrid's most exuberant month was May, when the city came spectacularly into its own. The weather was perfect, but not suffocating or too hot. The intense colours of the flower-beds encompassing each fountain, and the immaculate lawns running parallel to the central *paseos* of the Castellana and Recoletos, all looked more glorious than ever as terrace bars sprung up at every corner for the summer season.

Madrid celebrated 1 May just like the rest of Europe, but then also slowed down the next day for Dos de Mayo, too, a celebration of that day in 1808, when the *Madrileños* (presumably still all wearing their tunics) rose up against Napoleon, an event Goya immortalised in his painting, *The Charge of the Mamelukes*. Then the city celebrated its patron saint's day, *San Isidro*, on 15 May, and the whole week turned into a continuous party. Weekends started on Thursday and didn't end until Tuesday night. Dance displays and concerts were held every night all over the city, with stalls offering *Madrileño* delicacies and giant *cocido* stews for the crowds in the Plaza Mayor, while young and old dressed up in traditional *castizo* attire and headed down to Las Vistillas, the park near the Royal Palace, where makeshift stages hosted flamenco and salsa shows. Meanwhile Las Ventas held bullfights every day for a full month, all part of the San Isidro festival, a celebration of one day, extended for no apparent reason other than for the sheer fun of it, into thirty days. Naturally, that first spring, I joined in.

Daft not to.

As everyone else in the office seemed to be partying, I decided that if I couldn't beat them, I *had to* join them. Forget the fact that I was supposed to be taking on huge responsibilities in managing myself at my own new desk. I decided to become a 'people-manager' instead, which meant that I allowed all my staff (i.e., *me*) to enjoy the best of the calm before the storm, and to go on a few more jolly *marchas* before knuckling down to the job in hand.

As Chantal seemed to be still permanently stuck in the middle of her law exams (possibly just avoiding me), things started to get a little complicated again on the Satan's den front. Judith, the short, dark, rather hairy Mexican lawyer, took me out on the town during all the San Isidro festivities with her sister, María, also a bit hairy, and who introduced me to another *Madrileña* friend of hers *also* called María, who introduced me to several more of her own friends, including – yes – another María.

Because I soon found myself in a permanently semi-paralytic state, I lost sense of everyone's surname, and ended up simply numbering the Marías. Judith's sister, therefore, became 'María *Uno*', María *Uno*'s friend 'María *Dos*', and her friend 'María *Twes*'. I felt guilty about addressing them as if they were makes of cars until they started calling one another, *Uno*, *Dos* and *Twes* as well.

Our non-stop partying took us from the chic cocktail bars in the Castellana to a wild circuit of clubs – from Archy, Pachá and the melancholic Café Central jazz café in the Plaza del Ángel to the throbbing El Sol dive in Jardines, the place to go to last. Madrid was a village compared to London, and I soon found myself recognising and being recognised by an increasing number of doormen, boozily shaking their hands as the girls jumped the queues to get us effortlessly inside.

On one such weekend, we downed endless cocktails at the wood-panelled Cock bar in the Calle de la Reina and the Museo Chicote in Gran Vía before heading to Almonte in Juan Bravo, an authentic Sevillana club, where we were led straight to dance-floor-front tables whilst Judith and the Marías practised their Sevillana and flamenco moves. A few hours later, we somehow ended up together again on the Sunday for a marathon roast binge at one of Madrid's historic taverns, Botín in Cuchilleros, before aiming to hit the bullfight at seven o'clock, stuffed with rich, fatty food, and flushed from over a vat or two of Rioja and *pacharán*.

Between Botín and the bullfight, however, I insisted that I needed a brief *siesta* back at the turquoise *apartamento* after all the non-stop partying. Because I was the one who lived centrally, Judith and María *Uno* decided to come back with me. I wondered, albeit wearily and without great enthusiasm, what the Spanish Federation of Sexology Societies' statistics were on threesome-shagging during the *siesta*. I imagined there was very limited data. How did anyone have sex at all, I wondered, *ever*, when you spent the whole time (when not eating or partying) feeling pissed, bloated and exhausted? I crashed out on the large single bed with the usual prayer that it wouldn't catapult back up and squash me against the turquoise wall, as Judith and María *Uno* stretched out on the sofa and flicked through a couple of *Vogues* while watching TV with the sound turned down. I was just dropping off when the phone rang.

I opened one eye and saw María *Uno* pick up the receiver.

'*Si,*' she said. 'Hello?' She looked towards me on the bed. I waved a finger at her. I was shattered. I didn't want to speak to anyone. 'He's sleeping,' she continued. 'Who is this?' She covered the phone and mouthed a name to me.

Who? Oh – *Jesus, no!* – not my so-called ex-girlfriend calling from England again! I covered myself beneath the turquoise pillows.

'Well,' explained María *Uno*, all matter-of-factly. 'He's sleeping on the bed.' There was a pause. 'Yes, the bed,' she said again. This was obviously what was meant by a Mexican stand-off. 'Yes, I am in the same room,' she went on. 'Yes, he's on the bed in the same room. Yes … yes. Well, look, wait, let me pass you to –'

'No!' I whispered loudly, waving her away frantically. 'No, not me!'

'– to Judith,' said María *Uno*. 'She speak better English than me.'

I couldn't even begin to imagine the impact this was having on my ex back in England as Judith took the phone. Not just one girl in my room, but two! And *Mexicans*! It was irrelevant that they were hairy.

'Who's this?' said Judith, and … *giggling*. This was not good. 'Yes,' she said again. 'Yes, on the bed. Yes, that was María number one. Yes, number one. Well, I think *Teeem* knows many other Marías, too, so he just numbers them …'

'*Oh, Jesus Christ!*' I thought. There was a long pause. Then:

'Oh,' said Judith. 'Oh. Oh. I didn't know that. Well, we were just having a little *siesta* before the bullfight. *No*, you don't understand …!'

Even *longer* pause, then: 'Yes, I'll tell him. Yes, I've got it. Yes, I'll remember exactly what to say. Well, I don't blame you. I understand. I'd feel exactly the same. Yes. Goodbye. *Ciao-ciao.*'

Click, silence, then more giggles.

'What did she say?' I asked, plucking up the

courage to peek out from underneath the turquoise pillows.

'You don't want to know.'

'*Yes, I do!* There's no hope of a sodding *siesta* now! What did she say?'

'Well,' started Judith, slowly reciting it all from memory. 'She said you're a sick, cunt-struck, fat bastard and she hopes you'll die a slow death. Oh, and she'll never speak to you again.'

And she never did. Ever. Which solved that little problem.

Anyway, because it was obviously becoming clear that I couldn't even enjoy a quiet *siesta* in my own turquoise *apartamento* at the Colón any longer, I resolved to get out of there once and for all, and even more so once the claustrophobic summer heat *really* arrived. I needed to find my own flat.

13

I'm the first to admit that being an Englishman in Madrid in the late eighties and early nineties meant that I had a head-start on at least giving the impression that I was very busy and very important. And being busy and important was very much in fashion in Spain then, as it still was in Thatcher's Britain. Despite my minimal grasp of their language, I felt ahead of the Spanish merely because they let me, and they let me merely because I was English. They knew the 'you-pee' era had already triumphed in London, and they assumed I'd already lived through it and knew the ropes. The 'Winter of Discontent' and 'Crash of '87' were irrelevant. There wasn't a recession *here*, in Spain – not yet – and that was all that mattered. The fact that Condé Nast was American-owned, that I therefore spoke the language of our owners, that I'd lived and worked in London, the home of such illustrious media organisations as Saatchi & Saatchi, where men dared to wear bow-ties and appeared in *Campaign* magazine, week in, week out, leaning against their Porsches and BMWs ... well, I only had to don a blue and white stripey shirt, cufflinks and a polka-dot red tie, and I wasn't only accepted, I was looked up to by my colleagues in Madrid. It didn't matter that my Beaujolais-stained tie was from the Oxford Circus Tie Rack, or that my grey flannel double-breasted suit with the threadbare crutch was from Take Six and not Harvie & Hudson. I just looked the part. I looked English. I couldn't help it.

But whilst my clothes were English, my bushy hair let me down. It had a life of its own. It stood out wildly against a whole new breed of slicked-back-hair bankers and businessmen, all adopting the *'gomina'* look epitomised by the king of the 'you-pees' himself, a vain smoothie called Mario Conde, the young chairman of Banesto Bank, who turned out, in due course, to be a slippery *and* corrupt. *Gomina* was hair-lotion and *goma* was glue, although it was easy for me to confuse the two and it looked as if Spanish businessmen did, too. Their hair always appeared meticulously greased back, always curling slightly in the nape of the neck.

You only learnt what a haircut was in Spanish when you needed one, and then you soon learnt the difference between *cortarse el pelo*, which meant 'to cut your hair', and *tomar el pelo*, which meant 'to take the piss'. It was cruel mix of words for a *guiri* to learn, and whenever I asked my local barber with garlicky goatbreath to *tomar mas pelo* – or rather, what *I* believed to mean, 'to take more hair off' one particular suburb of my bushy head – I was unwittingly asking him to *really* take the piss. And invariably he did.

But then I found a solution. I'm not sure what came over me, but one day I decided to emulate the 'you-pees'. I plastered my hair down with *gomina 'extra-fuerte'* – extra strong. With my flattened, poncy new hair, I started to believe in the image the Spanish seemed to want me to have. Whenever I mentioned my squalid flat in Brixton to colleagues, Brixton became Fulham. I cringe at the thought of it, but I found I started to want red braces and one of those impossible-to-use Philippe Starck lemon-squeezer things, too, *and* a white XR3i Cabriolet. It would have to be white. I just needed a 'you-pee' flat to go with it all.

My lunchtime Spanish teacher, Beatriz, offered to combine my lessons into a flat-hunting exercise as a way to expand my vocabulary. However claustrophobic it had been in the turquoise *apartamento*, I'd also been spoilt rotten living so centrally. While work colleagues battled for space on the *metro* or on an *autobús* in standing-still traffic, I'd been able to simply stroll across to Serrano each morning, taking in a *café* and croissant in one of the numerous bars along the way. Each evening I'd taken the same stroll back, polishing off a *cerveza* or two at my local, the Espejo, to break up the gruelling three-minute journey. As I didn't own a car yet, one of my first stipulations to poor Beatriz as she started to asterisk potential viewings in *Segundamano*, the weekly free-ads paper, was that the flat had to be within walking distance of the office.

An ideal dream flat for any bachelor in Madrid is an attic flat with a roof terrace – *un ático con terraza* – just like out of Pedro Almodóvar's *Mujeres al Borde de un Ataque de Nervios (Women on the Verge of a Nervous Breakdown)*, which was successfully doing the rounds at the time. Somewhere to enjoy the Madrid light and throw parties as the sun set.

María Teresa, however, tried to talk me out of it: 'Oh, you don't want an *ático*, they're too noisy – and put your tunic back on immediately,' she said, or something similar that rhymed. But I didn't care about the noise. I just wanted light, sun, warmth and views. But when Beatriz and I set off to view places together, I soon discovered that you had to be one *taco* short of a *tortilla* to think *áticos* in the centre of Madrid were easy to find. Beatriz corrected my Spanish as I tried to discuss terms with confused landlords, eyeing us both suspiciously as we searched high and wide, off the exclusive area of the Plaza de Oriente with views of the Palacio Real, and in the old quarter, near the Plaza Mayor, as well as anywhere near Sir Rhino Twes.

While my flat-hunting vocabulary improved, Beatriz's own language skills were soon recognised by Lisa, the fashion director, and she abandoned teaching me for a full-time, glamorous coordinating job within the *Vogue* fashion department.

I was soon advised by Giovanni, *El Principe*, to employ the services of Peggy González, who'd lived near the Madrid Ritz Hotel for decades, and discreetly offered to find flats for *guiri* executives like me. Peggy was big, round, slow, great fun, softly-spoken, but a no-nonsense lady who also quickly told me to forget an *ático*. Instead, she immediately found me a flat in an elegant old apartment block with a courtyard behind big gates, in Calle Lope de Vega opposite the Prado Museum. On the first floor with an *interior* view, it was about as far from an *ático* as you could get. But I loved it.

Peggy was very clever. She showed me the flat at noon on a hot, sweltering day, making me walk very slowly alongside her in the scorching sunshine with my tunic still on. By the time we reached the cool, shaded, cobblestone courtyard of the apartment block, where water trickled gently from a tiny fountain amidst all the climbing plants – rosy-pink carnations, geraniums, jasmine and bougainvillaea (at last – *bougain-bloody-villaea!*) – all spilling out of huge ceramic pots and tumbling down from the balconies, and where classical piano music could even be heard from an open window, I was sold before I even entered the flat itself.

There *was* sunlight but it didn't beam directly into my flat – which was perfect, said Peggy, because it would be nice and cool in the summer. It had highly polished wooden floors, albeit very creaky, two bedrooms, a refurbished kitchen with a stylish black-and-white chequered floor and a bathroom decorated with ornate Spanish tiles. It had huge windows with shutters, a sprawling white stone bookshelf in the main living-room and a number of beautiful details in the door handles, skirting-boards, cornices and light fittings. It was semi-furnished, too, and as the few possessions I had in Brixton still hadn't joined me in Madrid, my vocabulary soon started to include words for essential household objects I needed to purchase, such as a corkscrew, ice-tray, wine-cooler and a lilo bed. Not only was the flat walking distance to the office, it was one of the most beautiful fifteen-minute walks in Madrid. The Prado Museum opposite was to become a second home, and my new life in Spain was suddenly beginning to look even better than I'd ever imagined. I moved in just in time for my first frenzied summer in the city.

14

In Madrid, the long, hot, dry summer brings endless, glorious daylight, all-night *marcha*, regular days lived at forty degrees, a number of dazzling bullfights, and the summer 'intensive work hour', the *hora intensiva*.

'Repeat after me,' started María Teresa, somewhat over-excitedly, *'Cuánta madera roería un roedor si los roedores royeran madera?'*

What this all meant was: 'How much wood would a rodent gnaw, if rodents would gnaw wood?' It came out of my mouth, of course, as the Spanish equivalent of, 'Wodents wawwing wood', which made María Teresa wet herself. She'd been trying to get me to say *trabajo* (work) and *tres horas* (three o'clock) properly. But it was no use.

'Anyway, it's too hot to work after three,' she said, regaining her composure.

'No, it's not.'

'*Sí, sí.* That's why we do the *hora intensiva*. Repeat after me: *hora intensiva.*'

The *hora intensiva* was adopted by many companies in Spain during the summer – which really meant working from eight until three without a lunch-break. The idea was to have lunch *after* three, followed by a long *siesta* until the evening. The tradition of this came from the factories and construction sites, where it genuinely *was* too hot to work in the afternoon sun. I couldn't understand the logic in it for an air-conditioned office. But no sooner had I been allowed to finally take off my tunic, than I was being told it was too hot to work after three. According to María Teresa, the staff just *had* to have their *hora intensiva*. Maybe the air-conditioning was only programmed to work summer hours as well.

As soon as the summer really took grip, thousands of sad Spanish men became abandoned in the city. They were referred to as '*Los Rodríguez*'. Whilst a *Rodríguez* continued to work during the week, his wife and kids migrated to the beach or the *sierra* for nearly three long months of vacation. He'd normally join them, guilt-stricken and blurry-eyed, from Friday night until Monday, and sometimes longer during August. Despite looking old and lecherous amongst all the nubile *Madrileñas* also left alone in the city, a typical *Rodríguez* would spend his nights cruising the Castellana terrace bars in the hope that he might just strike it lucky.

During July and August, I knew some people who

would start work just before eight and work until three, possibly taking coffee breaks but never lunch. At three, they'd leave the office and have lunch, starting to eat at three-thirty and finishing at five. They'd then go home and sleep until ten before going out for dinner. They'd arrive to eat at somewhere trendy at eleven, finishing at one in the morning. They'd *then* go to a couple of terrace bars, taking them to two-thirty, and then the first nightclub – which took them to five in the morning – and then a second nightclub – which didn't even *open* until five, but where they'd stay until seven – before going directly to the office where they would shave, change and start work again by eight.

My own body-clock couldn't handle that just yet.

In fact, while *Madrileños* had learned to stay indoors when the sun was out and then party after dark, my digestive system endured pandemonium trying to tag along. It had taken me seven months to get used to not having lunch until two, but now they wanted to push it back further. It wasn't only unfair, it was bloody dangerous. An Englishman is *not* supposed to function from eight until three on just coffee, and from half-noon onwards I was constantly having to apologise for the crescendos of persistent gurgling in my belly.

My own day went something like this: I'd wake up in a daze at the Lope de Vega flat, stuff down a stale croissant or two, then stagger to the office by eight. I wired myself with nonstop black coffee all morning, so much so that, when the clock struck three o'clock, it was like waving a red rag to a bull on speed. Palpitating with hunger and with my stomach bellowing out a bossa nova, I finally headed for 'lunch' back at my flat or in one of the cafés en route. Because I was always so ravenous by the time I found somewhere, I'd scoff umpteen bread rolls before any real food was placed in front of me, washing them all down with *cerveza*. And even during the summer I couldn't resist some real *Madrileño* cuisine – a *'cocido'* of chickpeas, cabbage, leeks, turnips, onions, pig's trotters, *chorizo* and *morcilla* at La Bola Taberna, for example – and then end up with *Madrileño* dog-breath all afternoon, punctuated only by a whiff of the aniseed-flavoured *pacharán*.

And sod the *siesta!*

At four-thirty, I'd go back to the office. What else was there to do? I couldn't sleep at that time of the day, with the sun shining so brightly. But then at six o'clock, when everyone was still asleep or gently stirring, and as the shops were just starting to pull open their shutters again, I'd go for a beer – just like I would back in England. I could delay my eating but not my drinking. I tried, but it was impossible. So I'd reward myself with a beer or two before seven o'clock, then wine from then on, which meant that by the time I finally met up with someone at ten o'clock, I was invariably half-cut. But I'd still carry on to all the terrace bars and night-clubs right through until three or four in the morning for fear of missing out on something. Summer for me in Madrid was mayhem.

Then there was the *'operación salida'* ...

'Are you ready for the *operación salida?*' María Teresa kept asking.

'What bloody operation?' I wondered. What had I done wrong now? My tunic was off and I was busy knuckling down and doing the *hora intensive,* even though my guts were all over the place. Now it seemed María Teresa wanted to operate on me. There'd been no mention of this in my contract of employment. I'd realised something was up as we entered the last week of July. Suddenly, everyone in the office was working twice as fast as normal. No sooner had the August issue of *Vogue* been printed and delivered on time, than the September issue was all but ready to print as well. And then finally, on 1 August, together with forty-degree temperatures, the *operación salida* arrived…

And everyone buggered off!

Operación salida, it transpired, meant the 'evacuation plan'. I'd never seen so many *Madrileños* trying to get out of the city in one go, and especially not on the same day. I couldn't understand why they didn't spread their *salida* operations over several days, but oh no, they just *had* to all set off together, even if it meant sitting in traffic for hours before they could finally get out of the city itself. From 1 to 31 August, when the *'operación retorno'* came into action and they all reappeared on exactly the same day again, Madrid was void of most *Madrileños*, all off taking the biggest bloody *puente* they could possibly take, and leaving just me, a skeleton staff, and all the sad, rampant *Rodríguez* behind.

But whilst hot, summer in Madrid could also be

beautiful. The *hora intensiva* came into its own as life became semi-nocturnal. Activity wound down, there was less traffic, more parking spaces, and even *taxistas* were less aggressive. To help me both work and party all hours, Luis (who left for Brazil in August) had finally rewarded me with my own secretary assistant – the bilingual Elena de Miguel, appropriately the first one to have ever greeted me when I arrived. As Elena had already taken her holiday earlier in the year, we took it in turns to man the office and keep things ticking over.

It was during this first long August that Chantal and I found the time to go away together at weekends and explore the Spain outside Madrid. With the Gypsy Kings blaring from Chantal's tatty Peugeot, we headed off to the greenery of Aranjuez, an hour's drive away. We didn't set off until late, so my hopes of a tour of the eighteenth-century royal palace were knocked on the head by lunch. We ate outside under the green awnings of a terrace restaurant, drinking gentle *sangrias* followed by chilled rosé wine, rattling in buckets of melting ice alongside us. We ate grilled sardines and pork chops, with large salads overflowing with tomatoes, soft-boiled eggs, olives, *espárragos* and onions generously tossed with vinegar and olive oil. We followed it all with the local speciality of giant strawberries and cream, before iced coffee and the inevitable *pacharáns*. Old men played *petanque* under the shade of the riverside trees nearby, where we later found a cool spot to watch them until about half-six, when they started to make their way to the eighteenth century *plaza* for a bullfight, and we headed reluctantly back to Madrid.

The relationship continued. We got drunk. It blurred things – boozy pilgrimages over long weekends to far corners of Spain, just to be getting out of Madrid for the night, sometimes to coincide with a village *fiesta*, in fact any excuse to see more of that fabulous country.

We saw Chinchón together, forty kilometres south of Madrid, with its picture-postcard Plaza Mayor, which doubled up as a bullring for their *fiestas*. We went as far as Seville, drinking and eating too much among the orange trees in its courtyards and jasmine-scented *plazas* by day, then hitting the riverside bars by night. But then finally, on a trip to Granada, some 400 kilometres south of Madrid, I plucked up the courage and chose probably the most romantic setting in Spain to break the most unromantic news to Chantal.

We'd arrived at the ornate, Moorish-style Alhambra Palace Hotel at noon on a Saturday. The Alhambra itself was breathtaking. After drinks watching the sunset reflect against the peaks of the Sierra Nevada, we took a taxi to a restaurant called Mirador de Morayma, a beautiful old house in the Albaicin, where we were led to a small balcony for an *aperitif* to watch the Alhambra floodlights slowly illuminate. The view was magical. We ate exquisite food in the achingly romantic, candlelit garden, but I suddenly had that hideous feeling of being in the right place at the right time with the wrong girl. I couldn't help it. I tried to explain.

And that was that.

But by then I had met Adolfo – or 'Adolf' – half-*Madrileño*, half-Venezuelan, hyper and hot-blooded. Dark and handsome, with chiselled features and permanent stubble, he made up for what little hair he had on top by being hairy everywhere else (at least that was visible), like some *Latino* Sean Connery. He was strong, stocky, with a bull neck and broad shoulders.

'*Hay mucho mas* sexy sea-bass in the Med,' he'd said.

Which was his Spanglish way of telling me that there were plenty of other fish in the sea. Unlike the perpetually rampant Adolfo, however, who sold billboard advertising by day but transformed himself by night into a hugely successful trawlerman, I was adrift in a poxy pedalo and didn't have a clue how to fish them out.

But Adolfo promised to show me the way with one of his many theories on how best to approach the *señoritas*, and – helped along by no end of tequila slammers – to hit what he called their 'wet spots'.

15

'*All* Madrid womans want love,' explained Adolfo, gulping wine.

'*All* womans?'

'*Todos.*'

He was dressed in light, baggy, cheesecloth chinos, no socks, and a bright, yellow-and-black patterned Hawaiin shirt. As I still hadn't invested in a *Madrileño*-style summer wardrobe, I was in heavy, wind resistant twill trousers, thick socks, and my so-called Marks & Spencer 'weekend' shirt – a frayed, hot, itchy-Clydella job. I might just as well have been wearing a heavily woven monk's habit. Adolfo looked tanned, fit and fertile. I didn't. I'm English. We were as different as the chalky white cliffs of Dover and a tasty bit of Manchego cheese.

We were in the fun, crowded El Cuchi Mexican restaurant, a somewhat touristy trap near the Plaza Mayor with a sign outside proclaiming 'Hemingway never ate here'. I'd let Adolfo order the food, and along had come an array of *tacos, quesadillas, fajitas* and *nachos* to set us off. His Latin American tastebuds were evident. My tastebuds were charred. I had eaten exactly what Adolfo had recommended to get my serpent perked up. This meant a cauldron of black bean hot chilli with *jalapeño* concoctions, which got me palpitating and sweating so fast, I felt and looked like I'd been stamping flamenco in a sauna with a pneumatic drill in each hand. My shirt was drenched. Adolfo looked calm, cool, dry.

I'd known Adolfo for several weeks now, but he obviously thought it still polite to suggest *guiri* venues such as this Mexican restaurant. I'd met him through Chantal. He'd first appeared one night when there was a whole crowd of us out, although I never knew whether this had been planned or whether we'd just bumped into him, which was typical in Madrid. Different groups of friends had always tagged along intermittently during each stretch of heady *marcha*, and as I'd never understood what the hell was going on, I'd often yelled *adiós* to someone leaving one bar only to be reintroduced to them in a nightclub an hour later for a second innings of debauchery. One minute I'd be in a throbbing *terraza* on the Castellana, the next I'd be squashed into a taxi with complete strangers riding convoy to a club. I think Adolfo was actually the ex-boyfriend of Chantal's sister, and the ex-boyfriend of most of her girlfriends, too – or so he claimed.

'*Todos* womans want love,' he said again, waving for the bill.

Adolfo spoke peculiar English, but not as peculiar as my Spanish, and somehow we found a way to understand every third word one another said in a combination of Spanglish and sign-language. He'd been explaining his theory that men had to understand how women *also* wanted to fall in love, and so the very first moments 'we men' spent in their company were crucial. You had to get as close as possible from the word go, he'd said. And the best way to do *that* was with *salsa* …

'I beg your pardon?'

'*Venga* – come,' he said, pushing his chair back. 'Where we go now, you no need speak Spanish. You no need speak at all. Just dance …'

'Adolf,' I said. 'I *can't* fucking dance.'

I had wrongly assumed that the Mexican meal would be the end of the evening and I had paced myself accordingly. It was gone one in the morning and I was dripping wet and steaming from the tequila on top of all the *cerveza* and Rioja from our pre-dinner *marcha*. But I couldn't let Adolfo down, and sure enough, we ended up at some hot, mad *salsa* club on the outskirts of Madrid. The smell of sweat, smoke and booze hit me as soon as I staggered in, and I could feel the chilli juice seeping from my pores. But I'd never seen so many sexy women dancing tightly and wriggling their butts – all doing *mambos* and *rumbas*.

A Load of Bull

'Cuban motions,' yelled Adolfo, or at least I think that's what he yelled.

Then he vanished! – out onto the dance-floor himself, leaving me with the *salsa* totty propping up the bar once I'd squelched my way through for a Mexican beer.

Adolfo danced expertly, of course, as any Venezuelan might, but watching him wriggle away with the first girl he closed in on, it looked as if he'd known her all his life. He was virtually mounting her. *This* was what he meant by getting close.

Adolfo had warned me about possible transvestites on the way over, and although the girl beside me was tall, dark, clean shaven, and smelt of a fusty blend of Ralgex and Old Spice cologne, there was no way she was a bloke. And I *know*, because I circled her several times before plucking up the courage to say something. She wore a red polka-dot blouse with a black bra bursting through, brimming with a wonderful set of maracas. They were definitely *real* tits. When I finally started a conversation, which consisted of me pointing towards the dance-floor to show how well my best *'amigo'* danced, she looked at some distant point beyond my shoulder, but not towards the dance-floor at all. Finally, she screamed, or gave the sound females do when someone more interesting arrives, then swept past me and was gone.

Adolfo, having witnessed this setback, dragged me out onto the dance-floor alongside two voluptuous Latin-looking *señoritas* and was now beckoning me to emulate his 'Cuban motion' wriggling, obviously with the aim of mounting the one *he* wasn't trying to mount. It was an utter disaster. As Adolfo and the girls wriggled their perfectly-formed hips, I didn't know what part of me to shake. I hunched myself double, trying to see if my hips were moving properly, but I couldn't even find them. I looked like Quasimodo attempting the cancan. The gluey *gomina* that had previously plastered my hair down was now matted with *jalapeño* chilli, tequilary sweat. When I looked up again, my *señorita* had wriggled safely away.

The music was still loud as I headed into the gents. There was pee all over the floor, with the basins blocked, and taps left running. Someone had trashed the place. It looked dubiously constructed, too – *so* dubious in fact, that I could still make out silhouettes on the dance-floor, jiving away through the thin walls. Some of the cubicles were occupied. I went into the last one in the row, leaving the door open. Desperate to relieve myself, I quickly unbuckled my trousers and leant my arm out for support against the side construction. It started to tilt, slowly at first, but then suddenly the whole partition gave way under the weight of my arm. I was already peeing but I lost balance. I pushed the cubicle wall into the next one which crashed into the next one, the whole crappy construction collapsing like a pack of cards! As I made a hasty retreat, someone screamed, 'Fuck! An earthquake!'

A Load of Bull

I saw Adolfo out on the dance-floor, unbuttoning his Hawaiin shirt and thrusting his hairy nipples towards the *señorita* he was also still shaking his arse at. She liked that. The next time I looked over, they were eating one another. I left them to it and staggered out to find a taxi.

16

My appreciation of Spanish art fuelled by the Royal art collections of the Prado, which I was able to frequently visit during the summer – and indeed my appreciation of all things Spanish – started to become obsessive. Seeing *guiri* tourists sunning themselves in their shorts and T-shirts, backpacks and baseball caps, I started to realise that Madrid had already changed me. When I'd first arrived, I, too, often sunbathed in the Retiro park until my face was on fire, or until Chantal had explained that it was a very naff (*hortero*) thing to do. Spaniards never sunbathed in their city parks, she said, and they only ever really took their shirts or tops off at the swimming pool or beach.

This rammed the point home to me that I didn't own a swimming pool and nor was I anywhere near a beach, the two prerequisites for any sane person wanting to come to Spain in the first place. So I decided to get my revenge through irony and turned my Lope de Vega bathroom into a kitsch shrine of typically Spanish souvenirs. I hung castanets from the mirror above the basin. I placed hideous little flamenco dolls and furry black bulls on the shelving near the loo. I pinned garish Spanish postcards into the sides of the mirror. I propped open Spanish fans and a matador hat on top of the bathroom cabinet together with a toy tambourine complete with all the red-and-yellow tassels. I draped a red-and-yellow Spanish flag alongside the towels. But my *pièce de résistance* lay on the back of the bathroom door, which was directly in front of you as you sat upon the throne. There, I had a bullfight poster with the names of El Cordobés and Paco Camino, with 'Your Name Here' in Spanish in the middle of them. I, of course, found this very funny indeed, even though it confused Spanish visitors to my flat, who assumed I believed *'Aquí Su Nombre'* was a real matador.

I think most Spanish visitors also assumed that I was genuinely into these souvenirs because they kept adding to the collection whenever they came round, although they often arrived with the real things instead of kitsch imitations. On one occasion, I was even presented with a pair of genuine *banderillas*, those coloured sticks used on the very top of a bull's withers during the second act of a bullfight. They're about seventy centimetres long and wrapped in brightly coloured red-and-yellow paper, with very sharp, harpoon-shaped steel points. Quite where I could put them in my bathroom without the risk of puncturing my scrotum, however, was unclear. I finally decided to hang them like crossbones high above the bathroom mirror with fat corks stuck on the ends. I was delighted. I was beginning to take the bulls seriously.

17

It was beginning to dawn on me that if I was to have any real future in Spain, I was going to have to become a *Madrileño*. Yet despite the fact I'd developed a healthy circle of colleagues and friends, had my own secretary and even Spanish *gomina* plastering my hair down, there were still plenty of obstacles in my quest to be a genuine local. And if I couldn't actually physically *become* a *Madrileño* overnight – I mean, if it was going to take time for me to get to grips with all the *puentes* and *horas intensivas*, or the increasingly heavy drinking and bingeing, or even the language barriers and late eating schedules – then I decided that I should at least absorb as much of the culture along the way as I could. In other words, do what any other self-respecting *Madrileño* would do.

Go and see a bull slaughtered by a bandy-legged grease-ball in pink tights and skintight pants.

I'd already been to the bullfight in Madrid – way

back in April, to celebrate my twenty-eighth birthday. It had fallen on a Sunday, and Las Ventas seemed to be holding bullfights every Sunday from then on. I'd decided to buy seven tickets and invite everyone I knew. I was more intrigued than anything else and had simply felt that it was something I needed to see. The bullfight I bought tickets for was a *novillada*, which meant that the bulls were lighter than normal and that the matadors were novice matadors, not world-class experts. I'd read that magic could still happen in a *novillada* as much as in a full *corrida*, though, and that one had to see a bad bullfight before one could appreciate a good one, if and whenever that happened. Real bullfighting fans, the true *aficionados*, would sit through hundreds of bad bullfights, living in hope of seeing something spectacular one day. When it happened, it remained with you forever.

In the end, it was Judith and her sister, María *Uno*, the hairy Mexicans, together with Francisco, Mayte, Jacobo and Sara from the office, who joined me at Las Ventas, Madrid's famous *plaza de toros*. I believe it was the first bullfight for most of the others, too, although Judith and María *Uno* had been several times in Mexico. They explained to me what was going on as we sat squeezed on cushions in our *tendido siete* seats – the 'number seven' area, partly shaded in *sol y sombra* and where the most critical *aficionados* sat, shouting abuse at the matadors risking their lives if they failed to produce any magic. We could see it all, good bulls and bad bulls, and I just fell in love with the whole atmosphere – the sand, the capes, the 'suits of lights', the parade, the cigar smoke, the smell of sherry, the cackling women fanning themselves, the gesticulating fat men in their short-sleeved shirts, the banter, the sun-creased old faces, the glamorous social set there to 'be seen', the carnations, the humour, the abuse, *everything* ...

By ten at night, in an old bar in one of the seedier areas of Madrid, I tried to come to terms with the exhaustion and mixed emotions of what I'd seen, of one minute being terrified for a matador, to being amused, disgusted, happy, sad, high, low and flushed in the sunlight.

Over the following months, the bullfight had started to more than intrigue me, helped by the fact that my patience was to finally pay off. I'd been going along most Sundays since April, often alone, and then suddenly I witnessed something extraordinary. Look, I'd never preach that the bullfight is right because I don't think it is. I don't think there's any justification for it at all. Whatever they say, bullfighting is almost certainly *wrong*, but it is a *fact of life*. The Spanish hold bullfights and will do so until ... well, until the cows come home. And something occurred which meant it would forever fascinate me.

It actually happened in the middle of a festival at Las Ventas, thanks to a matador from Seville called Manuel Ruíz Regalo, who they called the 'monkey-faced Manili'. Manili was normally a second-rate matador who fought with little art and no fear whatsoever, but what he did with the cape – more 'command' than elegance – caused my guts to churn over with fear and euphoria. Unlike the other two matadors on the day, Manili went out to greet his first bull by standing directly in front of the gate that the animal was about to charge from, with the cape held out to his right, yet *behind his back*. As the bull hurtled out into the ring with its lethal horns curled high and its nostrils flaring, Manili waited until it was almost on top of him before moving the cape from right to left – yet *still behind his back*. The result was that the bull changed direction at the very last split-second, jumping up and across the front of the matador's exposed body, and barely missing him. On the second bull, he did exactly the same thing again, but on *his knees*. This was either skill, art, insanity or all three, but either way, the crowd was immediately on its feet, including me.

This was a world and a spectacle I suddenly felt privileged to have glimpsed. As Manili worked his suicidal magic, Las Ventas hushed itself into a stunned and expectant silence, punctuated only with an ecstatic, sporadic chorus of *'Olés!'* If someone was to ask me later how I knew it was a 'good' bullfight, I wouldn't have known the technically correct thing to say, except that for *me*, the sheer 'beauty' of Manili's 'performance' was that I hardly noticed the bull at all. The animal was so close to the matador at each twist, twirl and turn that Manili seemed to be in absolute control of it, as if man and bull were one. They may have said he looked like a monkey, but I thought he was a genius.

At the end of the bullfight there was pandemonium in the *plaza* as he was carried around the ring and out through the main *puerta grande* gates *'en hombros'* – shoulder-high – waving the two bull's ears that he had been awarded. There were several spectators in tears around me, whilst total strangers embraced one another.

My growing passion for bullfights highlighted the distance that now existed between my old and new life. Invariably people who came to visit from England were dragged along to a bullfight they would hate. One such hapless guest, a schooldays sweetheart, was a dietician and vegetarian. What was I thinking? She detested it, even though we were seeing two fine veterans of the art, 'Antoñete' and Curro Romero. The last note I ever received from her ended with the words: '… and I'll never forgive myself for allowing you to take me to a bullfight.' The envelope was postmarked Melbourne, Australia.

18

Whilst Spanish *Vogue* was doing more or less OK, we got it wrong with our new decoration magazine, *Casa Vogue*, from the very first issue.

'Do you like it? *Te gusta?*' asked Luis, beckoning me into his office to show me the proposed launch cover of the décor title alongside two other versions that had been rejected. Ana and Giovanni, *El Principe*, were also there, both looking satisfied. The cover that Luis showed me was one of those minimalist jobs, showing a marble staircase with a cold, glass sculpture. There was nothing else: no rugs, curtains, fabrics, furniture, flowers, antiques, chairs – nothing at all.

'Not really, no,' I said, pointing to a different cover on the other side of his table. 'I prefer that one. It shows furniture, decoration …'

There was a silence as Luis slid it over. He looked up at me, nodding very gently as if in reluctant agreement.

The *Casa Vogue* that we launched was not only wrong because of the cover. The whole magazine was badly designed, full of illegible typography in clashing styles, arty pictures of uncomfortable executive chairs and impractical kitchen utensils, even steel bench-seats which would have looked perfect in a railway station waiting-room, but not in your average Spanish home.

It was the Italian influence, I was convinced. Luis, half-Italian himself, was being influenced by the opinions of too many Italians coming in and out of his office, including Giovanni, Ugo, the freelance fashion editor, and Rachele, our Milan correspondent. We relied on Italian furniture advertising, too, which soon dried up once the clients realised we were selling half as many copies as we'd originally predicted. In fact, *Casa Vogue* got to a delicate point after just seven issues where it didn't have *that* much advertising in it at all, except for Spanish porcelain floor tiles. And because finding homes to photograph was left to Giovanni and his regal network, the magazine always featured minor palaces, monasteries and diplomatic residences – totally bloody useless for your average Spaniard looking for decoration hints.

Soon, as a result of his friends' fear of being robbed or stung for undeclared taxable wealth, Giovanni ran out of castles to photograph. Instead, he latched on to anything that had charm, or where an architect or designer lived. With Madrid being the small world that it is, I soon discovered that my own apartment block in Lope de Vega was home to a couple of interesting characters – one being a famous architect and the other an art collector, who happily agreed to have their homes featured. But once Giovanni discovered that I lived in the same block, he asked whether my own pad was worthy of being photographed for the magazine, too ... 'to make up the trio'.

'A sort of British-style comes to Madrid apartment,' he waffled. 'To contrast against the other two – the Catalan architect and Parisian art collector ...'

'Are you kidding?' I cried. Images of my fetid loo with all those castanets, flamenco dolls, *banderillas* and 'Your Name Here' poster pinned on the door flashed through my head. 'That can never happen, Giovanni,' I added. 'Never.'

My neighbourhood, however, was certainly fit for the pages of *Casa Vogue*, especially the 'eating out' section. I'd soon discovered I was living in one of the most *cervecería*-saturated zones in the city. Practically every doorway in Calle de las Huertas led into a *taberna*. It felt very civilised to call in at La Fidula for a dry *fino* and olives on the way back to the flat, or at the Casa Alberto for an appetising *pincho* swilled down with a cold little tumbler of *vino tinto*. And the more I absorbed the Spanish way of life, the more I found myself speaking a tiny bit more of the language without having to mentally translate things first. I amazed myself with the ease in which I could now drop in and purchase a loaf of bread, fruit, *jamón* or *vino* at one of the scattered grocery stores or *bodegas* hidden between all the cafés, and I found that I'd even started to occasionally dream and think in Spanish, too. OK, it was still mainly sign-language Spanish.

Luis Carta's Ediciones Condé Nast had grown very fast, too fast. By November 1989, we'd already published twenty editions of *Vogue* and nine of *Casa Vogue*. A 'special projects' department had also been set up by Luis's wife, Ana-María, who'd finally joined us from Brazil. Special projects, *proyectos especiales*, were 'advertorials' – glorified advertising pages styled as editorial. We also started to create special supplements called *cuadernos* to package together with *Vogue* for sale at the news-kiosks. We had *cuadernos* for the catwalk shows, for menswear (*Vogue Hombre*), as well as for childrenswear and bridalwear. But it was clear we were overstretched. Just five days before we were due to print our January 1990 edition of *Vogue*, I was told by the demented José Manuel that there was an eight-page advertorial to add. Adding pages at the last minute was normal: but not when the pages weren't actually ready.

'They haven't even *started* on them?' whined Luis. '*Son tontos.*'

'*Son tontos*' meant they were 'silly'. *Silly?* They weren't silly, they were a bunch of lazy, lying, cretinous shysters. But I didn't say that. Besides, I sensed Luis had finally got the message: we needed to get organised.

Luis always liked to reshuffle things. Maybe he recalled my doubts about the very first cover of *Casa Vogue*, or the way I kept identifying the problems we had. Whatever it was, I suddenly assumed the very grand title of 'assistant publisher' on top of all the production chores, working directly with Luis himself in his role as 'publisher' of *Vogue* and *Casa Vogue*.

'Together,' said Luis, 'we'll put it right.'

And to share the work load, Luis found a colleague – a young Italian called Maurizio – to join my department.

Maurizio, or 'Morris', was twenty years old and the son of our Milan correspondent. He'd come to Madrid for a year to avoid the Italian military service. Luis had decided that it was a good opportunity for Morris to learn a bit about publishing and improve his English – so Elena, Morris and I started communicating with one another in 'Spanglitalianish':

'Morning, *Teeem*.'

'*Ciao*, Elena.'

'*Hola*, Morris.'

'*Tutto* OK?'

'*Todo* very *bene*.'

'*Fantastico. Ora*, I've got to *volare* to Valencia *con* Giovanni.'

Which was Spanglitalianish for, 'Fantastic. I've now got to fly off to Valencia with Giovanni …'

Each year Valencia hosted an International Furniture Fair, the *Feria del Mueble*. As part of *Casa Vogue*'s new strategy, it was decided that we should have a stand at the fair, and that we should host an extravagant party for all our clients. So Luis asked Giovanni and I to fly down to find a suitable venue.

I always felt humble in front of Giovanni. Because he looked like a king, he got treated like one. As we boarded the 8 a.m. flight from Barajas, I noticed the air-hostesses only had to glance at his boarding-pass and appearance before they were curtsying like crazy, guiding him gently towards the best front-seat on the plane before grumpily squashing me in alongside him, obviously assuming that I was his podgy bodyguard or butler.

Moments later, he was asleep and snoring. His eyeballs had rolled round the back of their sockets to reveal white and blue-blooded bulbs. His enormous Bourbonic nose, never-ending forehead and teeth were now all pointing up towards the air-conditioning and his noble tongue seemed to have nestled upon his majestic bottom lip. He didn't wake up until we hit the tarmac at Valencia airport, and only then suddenly jolting upright, as if ignited by electrodes.

We were met by 'Inmaculada', our advertising executive in Valencia. Inmaculada means 'Immaculate', and she did indeed have immaculate legs and an immaculate figure, as well as one of those striking, flat model faces with huge, cat-like eyes, like a Spanish Michelle Pfeiffer. She was gorgeous and it was difficult to take my eyes off her as she guided Giovanni and I around the city, helped along by a catering friend of hers called Manolo, all crammed into her tiny Seat, with Giovanni's crown of silver hair crushed against the greasy interior roof.

We started the day at Manolo's own restaurant with a coffee – or as Giovanni called it, a *'cafélito'*, which meant a 'little coffee'. I had finally learnt that this was known as an 'affective suffix'. Adding affective suffixes such as *'-ito'* and *'-illo'* to the end of nouns, adjectives or adverbs added emotional overtones depending on the mood – and Giovanni was very fond of them. *'Eres un comilón,'* for example, meant 'You are *such* a fat pig!', whereas *'Eres un comiloncillo,'* simply meant, 'You sure like your food!' Personally, I'd been advised by Beatriz to avoid using them until I was far more fluent in the language (i.e. never), since they could sound very silly or even insulting if misused. In some cases, she'd said, these diminutive forms were considered more appropriate in women's speech than men's, and they were often used when talking to little children. Needless to say, most Spaniards, and especially Giovanni, seemed to use them when talking to me all the time.

Exactly why Giovanni had this habit of affixing most gastronomic delights with a shrinking *'-ito'* was beyond me, especially as he made the *cafélito* last a good hour. As he downed a perfectly normal-sized beer, for example, it became a modest *cervezita*. A large glass of wine swiftly following it became a simple *vinito*. Throw in a generous *tapa* and it became a *tapita*, whilst a giant *paella* became a tiny *paellita*. And just like María Teresa, Giovanni also had a habit of reciting Spanish proverbs and tongue-twisters, then taking delight in seeing my reaction, or bursting into fits of regal giggles if I tried to recite them back.

His favourite was, '*Poquito a poquito Paquito empaca poquitas copitas en pocos paquetes.*' This meant, 'Little by little, Paquito packs a few tiny glasses into a few packages.' Giovanni would always utter it immediately after ordering another tiny '*-ito*' top-up of whatever it was he was drinking, as if justifying his alcoholic needs by pretending it was really little 'Paquito' who was doing all the drinking, little by little. He'd always pronounce it in that toothy articulated way of his, too, downing glass after glass of red *vinito* with his huge Bourbonic teeth slowly staining themselves to fruity red. It was a delight to watch.

'You've got the same name as the king!' exclaimed the waiter.

'My dear chap,' said Giovanni, rather startled. 'I beg your pardon?'

'Same name as the king!' cried the waiter, beckoning over his colleagues. 'Same name as the king!'

This was all very embarrassing. Here we were – 'Immaculate', Manolo, Giovanni and me – and the waiter had just taken Giovanni's credit card to settle the bill, only to notice the name on it: Juan de Borbón. It had been a long day and our flight back to Madrid left at six-thirty. Having started at Manolo's own stylish restaurant, a modern venue with an open-deck terrace overlooking the Valencia yacht club, we'd since been driven in the tiny Seat to visit six or seven other potential venues for the *Casa Vogue* soirée – including a jazz club, a ferry terminal, a monastery, a museum, a small palace – and now this very expensive *paella* restaurant on the beach front, where we'd enjoyed a mammoth lunch-*ito*.

'Look!' said the waiter to one of his colleagues, now also hovering over our table. 'He's got the same name as the king!'

'My dear chap,' said Giovanni, extremely politely and somehow not patronisingly. 'Do you not know the name of your own king?'

The waiter looked confused as Giovanni took a five thousand *peseta* note out of his wallet, keeping it half-concealed against his chest.

'Guess the name on this note, then you can have it,' said Giovanni.

The waiter grinned wildly and conferred with his colleague.

'Juan de Borbón!' he said finally. 'Just like you!'

'Juan de Borbón! Juan de Borbón!' nodded his colleague.

'No …' said Giovanni. 'If it *was* Juan de Borbón, then that *would* be me, because Juan is Spanish for Giovanni.' He showed them the note before tucking it triumphantly back into his wallet. 'Juan *Carlos* de Borbón,' he pronounced. 'Your king is Juan *Carlos* de Borbón.'

After several *pacharán-itos*, we eventually headed back to Manolo's yacht club restaurant and agreed that of all the venues we'd visited during the day, Manolo's would actually be the ideal place to hold the party. So we'd spent the whole day on a complimentary tour of the *tapitas* and *vinitos* of Valencia, when the answer had been right under our noses with the very first *cafélito* of the day. There it was again, the whole taking-years-to-come-up-with-a-final-decision thing. After a good forty-five minutes of *adióses* at Valencia airport, we finally settled on a date for the *fiesta*. (And when we hosted it months later, we did so in style, topping it off with fireworks to light up the harbour. The best pyrotechnicians in the world are Valencianos.)

So *Casa Vogue* was back on track, even though it cost us a fortune to keep Giovanni lubricated with gin-and-Dubonnet cocktail-*itos* on many more trips to organise things. Gin-and-Dubonnet, he kept telling me, was 'Your Queen Mum's favourite tipple', and I guess *he* should know, as he also kept telling me he'd mixed the old girl one too many in the past.

Giovanni was a source of constant amusement, though, and I often wondered if Luis simply took the piss out of him about his royal connections. On one occasion, I found Giovanni wandering around the offices at Sir Rhino Twes, looking embarrassed as he handed out sheets of paper. It was an 'inter-office memo' addressed to 'all staff', 'from Giovanni'.

The memo read: 'Last night I dined with the king.

He thinks the latest edition of *Casa Vogue* is excellent. He sends his congratulations to everyone.'

'Well, that's great, Giovanni!' I said, genuinely impressed.

'Yes,' he mumbled. 'I mentioned it privately to Luis. *He* made me write this.'

19

It was February 1990, and I was already living a double-life, juggling both the *Casa Vogue* and production work as well as trying to keep up with all the *marcha*. I'd enjoy a privileged preview of a trendy new club with Ana Puértolas, our editor, during the day, and then at night, until dawn, I'd be out on the piss with Adolfo at the same venue. One day I'd be trying to devise an advertorial for a group of Valencian furniture manufacturers, the next I'd be entertained over a long, boozy lunch by Clemens Brauer, the commercial director of our printer, whenever he visited us in Madrid …

Clemens was a moustached, well-built German with permanently smiling eyes. As we printed Spanish *Vogue* in Barcelona, Clemens always chose a Catalan-style restaurant to entertain me in Madrid.

'Ve zink it'z very good zat you are 'ere!' he always roared. 'It'z very good zat you have got zem to zend uz pagez on time. Printerz have zchedulez, too, you zee. AND ZCHEDULEZ MUZT BE KEPT!'

And then we'd go for ze lunch.

The first time we did this we went to Paradís, a Catalan restaurant with a mosaic-tiled floor, in the Calle Marqués de Cubas. Clemens took great delight in ordering ze very best red wine and watching my reaction as I savoured it.

'*Salud*, Clemens,' I said, thanking him for his hospitality. 'Cheers.'

'*Força al canut*,' he replied, chinking his own glass against mine. I didn't understand a word.

'I'm sorry?' I said. 'Alfonso Can-ooky who?'

'*Força al canut*. It'z zomething ve zay in Barcelona.'

'Alfonso Canute?' I said, sipping the wine. I assumed he was the President of Catalunya, or possibly the supplier of the superb wine.

'No, not Alfonso Canute. *Força – al – canut* …'

I tried it again but it still came out as Alfonso Canute.

'That'll do,' said Clemens, still smiling yet swiftly changing the subject. I was to make a toast to Alfonso Canute many times over the coming months, not knowing who the hell he was or what he was famous for. I would simply raise my glass to bemused Spaniards and say, 'Alfonso Canute!' – assuming it to be a perfectly polite thing to do. Then Daniel, the American banker, explained that *'força al canut'* was Catalan for the Spanish *'fuerza al canuto'* – meaning, 'strength to your penis'.

That first meal was a full introduction to Catalan cuisine. We started with the simplest but most exquisite Catalan invention of all, *pa amb tomàquet*, bread with tomato. I soon realised why our round table was so large. From the very first dish, our meal became a DIY gastronomic festival with all the spare space soon taken up. The waiters arrived with a large loaf of sliced bread, already lightly toasted. Alongside it, they placed a flask of cold-pressed olive oil together with some salt and a basket of small, deep-red tomatoes – wonderfully ripe and juicy.

Clemens led the way. He cut a tomato in half and rubbed it over a slice of the toasted bread, adding a long trickle of olive oil and a scattering of salt, just as the waiters placed an enormous oval plate of the very best *jamón ibérico* in the middle of the table as well. Now, I'd tasted *jamón* before, but not like this. This was the most exquisite, wafer-thin *jamón* ever – *pata negra*, he explained, which was the black trotter, the very best mark of the breed. Clemens delicately layed several wisps of *jamón* on top of the tomato and olive-oil soaked toast, then handed it to me. It melted in my mouth. Minutes later, the waiters flapped more napkins in front of us, but this time to wear as bibs. The great green onion feast was about to begin.

Calçots, the small, flavoursome green onions from the Valls area, explained Clemens, were a Catalan 'zpeziality' in February. They were being presented at our table on an enormous *terracotta* roof-tile. Alongside, a miniature grill was also set up, keeping a number of succulent pork chops sizzling sweetly under our craving eyes. Another waiter arrived with a chopping-board and a variety of long, thick, hard and soft sausages – from spicy peppery ones to smoked salamis and blood sausages, including *butifarra, chorizo* and *lomo* – an air-dried loin of pork. Delicious-looking dips were brought to fill up the remaining space on the table – a piquant almond and tomato sauce, as well as *aliolo*, garlic mayonnaise.

Clemens picked up a *calçot*, peeled back its charred skin with his fat fingers, then dipped the exposed onion into the sauces.

'Now,' he said, ensuring his bib was securely tucked into his neck. 'Vot you do iz ziz. You tip ze 'ed back and open ze mouth wide. Now hold one of ze onionz like ziz, you zee, with ze long white ztalk high above you, then bring it down between ze teeth like ziz …'

The *calçot*, dripping in sauce, disappeared down Clemens's voracious German throat.

'Alfonso Canute!' I said, raising my glass.

Our napkins were soon smeared with black stains from the charred onion-skins. We took it in turns to fork pork chops onto our plates and slice up *butifarra* and *lomo* on the chopping-board. It was one of the best lunches I'd ever had. At nearly five o'clock – *five o'clock* for crying out loud – I was reluctantly escorted out of the restaurant and back to Sir Rhino Twes, painfully holding in a barrage of potentially catastrophic *calçot*-induced farting.

Back in my office I tried to focus on the piles of

documents that were rapidly accumulating on it. I shut my eyes for just a brief second ...

Oh, Jesus Christ! It was gone six-thirty when I suddenly jerked awake to the sound of ringing! I thought it was my alarm-clock back at the Lope de Vega flat. I didn't know where the fucking hell I was! I snatched the phone, my impromptu *siesta* horribly over.

Concha, our new receptionist, told me there was a 'gentleman' in reception to see me. Adolfo had arrived in time to take me out.

Concha had only been working at Condé Nast Spain for a fortnight but, according to Adolfo, I should have buried my diabolical serpent deep into her satanic den '*ages* ago'. His theory this time? Her *name*.

'Concha' can mean 'shell', or 'oyster shell', but it is also short for a Spanish 'compound name' combining the Virgin Mary's *María* with *concepción* – *María de la Concepción* – meaning the Immaculate Conception. According to Adolfo, it also meant 'the fertile one', and someone permanently *en celo* – on heat. A bit like Adolfo himself.

I tried to keep Adolfo away from the Sir Rhino Twes offices as much as possible, but it wasn't easy. He was a self-confessed *señorita*-sniffer, and I'd actually begun to envy him. I'd also begun to wonder whether I should have ever ended my relationship with Chantal. Finding a replacement was much harder than I thought, but Adolfo said I simply needed to take the proverbial bull by the horns. He kept telling me that I was sitting on a goldmine of beautiful women where I worked, and it was true, but they weren't that approachable. And whilst Adolfo only had to wait in the reception area for a few minutes before he left with a new phone number (this time lucky Concha's), I didn't want to be seen as a lech around the office.

My guts were still gurgling with green onions, but after my office *siesta*, I'd felt refreshed enough to accompany Adolfo out on another *marcha*. We'd started in one of the alleys just below the Plaza Mayor again, near the Cava de San Miguel, where we'd already had several *cervezas* in some of the city's oldest taverns. We'd been serenaded by passing musicians and singers dressed in traditional Spanish costume of knickerbockers and waistcoats, who wandered around the area playing and 'passing the hat'. It was fun, and I could have stayed longer, but tonight, Adolfo had promised, would be different. Tonight, he'd said, I couldn't fail. I would be getting laid. He'd set me up with someone for a sit-down dinner – for 'the four of us' – and with someone, he promised, who spoke some English.

'Her name?' I asked, intrigued.

'Eligia.'

I couldn't pronounce it very well, but 'Eligia', Adolfo assured me, meant 'the chosen one'. The one *he'd* chosen for me.

'And yours?' I asked.

'Milagros,' came the satisfied reply.

Milagros meant 'Miracles'. Can you imagine

having a girlfriend called Miracles – I mean, having to say stuff like, 'Fancy a curry, Miracles?' and 'Morning, Miracles'? I'd never had the courage to tell Adolfo that his own name didn't have such great connotations, either. At least I had *one* up on him. I hadn't been christened Adolf Parfitt.

Anyway, the sexual appetite of Spanish women depended on their names, he'd told me, and his way of labelling the *señoritas* as 'unlikely', 'possible', 'probable' and 'definite' went hand-in-hand. Concha was (or would be) a 'definite', as indeed, no doubt, would be Milagros and possibly even Eligia. Girls who'd been lucky enough to be named Esperanza ('Hope', – i.e. hoping for it), Mayte ('Lovable' – obvious), Margarita ('Pearl' – ditto), and Bienvenida ('Welcome' – say no more) were all on Adolfo's 'definite' radar, whilst Dolores ('Sorrows'), Paciencia ('Patience'), Dominga ('Sunday') and Nieves ('Snowdrops') were all 'highly unlikelys'.

Over the months, Adolfo had also been busy explaining more to me about the true aspirations of young *Madrileñas* when it came to when, where, and with whom they might allow some horizontal rumba, and whether or not it could be achieved *before* marriage, or at least without a decade of Catholic courting beforehand. The *salsa* club had been a poor choice, he'd admitted, as the Latin American girls there didn't speak a word of English and didn't want to. Every Spanish girl wanted a husband, though, he'd said, but whether they'd really want to tie the knot with a tubby *guiri* was another matter. And if they had no intention of being in it for the long haul, they were highly unlikely to let me anywhere near their *'chinchillas'* at all. Sure, there were plenty of *Madrileñas* out there who craved an English tongue in more ways than one, but it had to be the right *type* of tongue. When I'd asked him what he meant, he'd said there were 'Englishmen and Englishmen' in the eyes of Spanish girls. At one end of the scale there were tattooed hooligans, and at the other end there were Tory MPs who dressed up in stockings and suspenders with satsumas up their arses. 'Or whatever else they could find,' he'd said. I didn't realise Britain had such an internationally tarred image. I vowed to improve my Spanish – which Adolfo agreed was vital – and we set off to several other bars.

Suffice to say that our pre-dinner boozy *marcha* went on so long that our quiet 'foursome' dinner was typically enough rearranged to include three other couples. Adolfo's date, Miracles, lived up to her name. Gorgeous, with dark, pleading eyes, romantic and sexually sizzling, she was the personification of Spanish sensuality. No doubt she would perform miracles in bed, but she looked like she'd be happy to start working wonders under the restaurant table if you let her. According to Adolfo, she was the sexual equivalent of a hot, tasty, readily available *tapa*. Eligia, the 'chosen one', the girl that he had thoughtfully tried to pair me off with, actually failed to show. She was, I learnt, 'working', which, I overheard from one of the smirking others, meant she was probably a hooker. As the only other single bloke at this rearranged mass dinner, I was introduced to the only other single *señorita*, a big lump called Soledad. *Soledad* meant 'Lonely', and I quickly got a sense of why she *was* lonely. She was not the sexual equivalent of a tasty *tapa*. As I drunkenly squashed myself in beside her, with our chairs pressed uncomfortably against the restaurant wall, I envisaged the sexual equivalent of bull's tail and tripe with dried prunes, onions, streaky bacon, diced carrots and garlic. I couldn't face it. And I suddenly realised that my lunchtime green onion banquet was threatening to explode from every orifice. If I didn't get the hell out of there, soon I was going to crop-spray poor Soledad.

At that point, Adolfo leant over and slurred something ridiculous to Miss Lonely, such as, 'Has he kissed you yet? He's a good kisser!', and that was the end of it. Big, buxom Soledad shoved her chair back in pure horror, and the full force of it trapped my finger against the wall.

'Jesus Christ! My fucking finger!' I screamed.

Everyone in the restaurant stopped talking and gazed over.

I could feel my guts caving in.

I scrambled to get out.

20

Condé Nast is owned by the Newhouse family and represents just a fraction of their interests alongside numerous regional daily papers and cable television in the States. The owner himself is Samuel I. 'Si' Newhouse Jr, born in 1927, the eldest son of the founding father Sam, himself the eldest of eight children of Jewish immigrants. He'd started out as an office boy on a New Jersey weekly paper. Years later, the story goes, he had given his wife not a subscription to *Vogue*, as requested for their wedding anniversary, but the Condé Nast company itself. Si Newhouse himself was known for his eccentric manners and showing up at society occasions in just a polo-shirt and sneakers. He was described as one or all of the following: shy, rude, awkward, brilliant, insecure, inarticulate, very short. Some even said that, when sitting down, his feet didn't touch the floor. *Fortune* magazine normally ranked the Newhouse wealth at $13 billion, give or take a few billion, with Si ranked as the most powerful, if not the wealthiest, man in the States.

Our new chairman was Jonathan Newhouse, thirty-seven, the son of Si's late uncle, Norman Newhouse. He'd gone through a succession of ascending jobs during the eighties, including stints on the *New Yorker* and *Details* magazine, but had now been moved to Paris to take on the chairmanship of Condé Nast's international operations. The fact that he'd been sent to Paris without any knowledge of the language meant that Jonathan's French was as disastrous as my Spanish.

He was a fun, but also odd, secretive, shy and complex character, *also* short, and when I met him in Madrid, he had thick, curly hair, round wiry spectacles, a bow-tie, braces, white shirt and a very odd-fitting dark suit, which seemed to be what he wore every day. With his protruding jaw bone, he looked more like a New York boffin-lawyer than the in-coming European chairman of an empire of glossy fashion magazines.

We met to discuss *Casa Vogue* and talked about how I'd come to Madrid from the London office (where I would never have had a one-to-one with the chairman) and joked about how bad my Spanish was and how bad his French was. Then I enquired what he thought of the latest *Casa Vogue* as I pushed a copy across and asked him to flick through it.

'Well, it's not really for me to say,' he replied, half-nodding and half-shaking his head. He seemed to do this a lot when unsure how to reply. 'What do *you* think about it?' he finally added.

'I think it's crap.'

'Crap?' he squeaked.

'Well, not *all* crap. But, you know, mostly crap.'

There was another awkward silence so I wondered if he really *did* know what I meant. So I started to flick through the magazine, indicating pages that didn't work very well. I explained how I thought it could be improved, where some photos should have been larger and others smaller, where cover lines and intros should have been more dynamic, and how the whole thing could have been made much more exciting visually. As I turned the magazine around to point out examples, he started to nod but said nothing else at all as I went through each page. I realised at that moment I'd become slightly obsessed by our magazines.

'Right,' he said, at the end of my manic presentation. 'I can see that it needs improving. So what plans do you have to do that?'

I told him that I thought it should become more about lifestyle and less about design and architecture. Also, because we'd had success with an issue dedicated to Valencia, I said that I thought we should do more special editions on Barcelona, Seville and Madrid in the build up to the '92 celebrations. Whilst Jonathan scribbled away furiously on his lined pad, I asked him if he'd been to Seville himself. He shook his head.

'Oh, you *must,*' I said. 'We should take you there. It's a fantastic city. And the *women* …'

There was yet another awkward silence. I noticed Jonathan doing those odd head movements again, as if he didn't know which way to look. Perhaps he was as shocked as I was that he was actually being invited somewhere, and especially by me.

After that first meeting, Jonathan would visit Madrid once a month. Each time Luis would take him to lunch in an old *'tipico' taberna*-style restaurant, such as Casa Paco or Casa Lucio, two of Madrid's best, and then invite a couple of us to join them. I got invited along quite a bit, often to accompany Giovanni, and soon discovered that Jonathan was obviously learning about Spanish eating habits the hard way like I'd had to. He was clearly ravenous by the time we ever went for lunch. Just like me, he'd immediately rip the bread rolls to shreds in a rush to get something into his mouth, scattering crumbs all over the place, much to the surprise of the refined gourmets, Luis and Giovanni.

Knowing he was hungry and impatient, Luis always ordered for him as soon as the waiter seated us, something made easy by the fact that Jonathan always knew exactly what he wanted: cheese, ham, sausage, then steak and chips, accompanied by a beer. So Luis always lined up some *queso manchego, jamón* and black sausage, and sometimes even a plate of fried eggs mixed up with chips, a delicious speciality of Casa Lucio, and something that both Jonathan and I could spoon into our mouths spectacularly quickly. On one occasion, he suddenly got the hiccups and decided that the best cure was to place his linen napkin over the top of his beer glass and drink the beer through it. The beer absorbed by the napkin proceeded to dribble down the sides of his suit. The hiccups continued.

I soon discovered that Jonathan enjoyed any sexual innuendo. On one occasion we were talking about the printer we used in Barcelona and whether or not there were any alternatives to get a better price. I explained that I'd visited a few potential suitors and started to list the names, which all sounded the same in Spain, such as Fotomatica, Fotocomposer, Rotagraphic, Rotafoto or the renowned Rotedic, pronounced *rota-dick*, which suddenly caused Jonathan to crack up.

'Rota *what?*' he spluttered through his food.

'Rota *dick*,' I repeated slowly.

'*No entiendo*,' said Luis, asking me to explain the joke in Spanish.

'Dick is *polla*,' I said. 'So it means *rota-polla*, like … er … like, Print-a-Prick.'

Jonathan spat out his food. I thought he was about to die laughing. Luis just smiled politely, although I still don't think he found it that funny. He then started to explain it all to Giovanni in Portuguese, and then Italian, because for some reason Giovanni had decided to not understand the joke, even though he spoke perfect English. Once it had been explained to him in several languages, Giovanni still didn't find it funny and even looked embarrassed. But Jonathan loved it and on every visit from then on, he'd try and slip 'Rotedic' into the conversation.

Luis's chauffeur, or *'chófer'*, was called Restituto, but for some reason he preferred to be known simply as Alonso. He drove the Condé Nast navy-blue Jag, and when he wasn't driving it, he was either busy polishing it outside Sir Rhino Twes, where it was permanently double-parked (thanks to the 'press' badge he'd scrounged out of the Madrid traffic authorities), or he was perched against the matronly María Teresa's desk, helping her to concoct tongue-twisters or wheeler-dealing some crafty scheme while waiting for his daily instructions.

No-one knew Alonso's real age but he was definitely getting on; and he was a lovely guy, despite looking like Franco. He was naturally very short, of course, as well as rotund, bespectacled and bow-legged, so it was a miracle how his feet even reached the Jag's pedals. He also had that Spanish spinning-top shape befitting the old brigade. In fact, if you wanted to compare the 'new' Spain with the 'old', then you simply had to stand Alonso next to someone like Carlos, the new twenty-year-old lad in the office. Alonso was elderly, short and cantankerous, whilst Carlos was young, happy and a gentle giant. Something had happened to the Spanish national diet towards the end of Franco's regime, so that the younger generation was much taller than their forefathers of only a couple of decades ago.

Alonso was always dressed impeccably, sometimes

in a heavy three-piece suit, despite the heat, and he often liked to pretend that Spanish Condé Nast was actually his own. On one occasion, according to Luis, when he accompanied him to Barajas airport to collect a very important person at the private jet arrivals gate, Alonso tried to physically stop the VIP from getting into the back of the car.

'Hey, you!' yelled Alonso, opening one of the doors of the Jag for Daniel, then still our chairman, but shouting across at the rumpled character in chinos trying to get into the other side. 'What the hell do you think you're doing?'

There was a silence and the jet-lagged passenger looked very confused.

'Alonso, this is Mr Si Newhouse,' explained Luis.

The time had come for me to buy a car, and this now being 1991 and me being thirty-one years old meant it would have to be one of those white Cabriolets. I'd adapted more to the *Madrileño* lifestyle. A white Cabriolet would fit my thrusting new image, and I was convinced it would even help me find the leggy blonde I was now aiming for. I'd decided upon a convertible white Volkswagen Golf GTi, which seemed to be on billboards everywhere in Madrid, and, like it or not, Alonso was going to help me buy one. But, *oh no* –

'You don't want one of those ...' began María Teresa.

'Why not?'

required, and so I ended up having to hand over 60,000 pesetas (some £300) less than expected. Then after Alonso and the dealer haggled away, I ended up receiving some extra special accessories, like rubber car-mats which weren't originally included, and even a VW cuddly-toy. Flushed with excitement, I would have given Alonso anything at all to thank him for his help – and that was exactly the state he was hoping I'd be in. His timing was perfect as we left the dealership and he casually asked me if I could possibly lend him the 60,000 pesetas that he'd 'saved' me because he hadn't had time to go to a cash-point.

'*Lend* it to you, Alonso?' I said, handing it over. 'You can *have* it.'

'*No, hombre* –'

'Yes, I insist, Alonso ... you've *done me proud* ...'

'No, I'll *borrow* it for now ...'

I never saw the money again, of course, but we became very good friends. And good old Alonso also scrounged another press badge out of the traffic authorities so I could end up double-parking the car anywhere I liked. Pretty flash for a *guiri*.

Soon I was as aggressive and noisy with the car horn as the *Madrileños*. In fact, car horns are a constant accompaniment in Madrid, with the *taxistas* the worst culprits – so much so that the definition of a split-second in Spain is the time it takes for a *Madrileño taxista* waiting behind you at traffic lights to sound his horn once the lights turn from red to amber, let alone green.

'Because it's too hot here,' added Alonso, per[ched] against her desk.

'That's exactly *why* I want one,' I said.

'No, it doesn't work like that in Madrid,' Alonso.

'What do you mean, "it doesn't work like that"?

'If you buy a convertible, you'll never have the down because it's too hot and noisy. You'll wa[nt a] normal car with air-conditioning, that's what y[ou] want.'

'No, I want a convertible.'

'No, you don't,' said María Teresa.

'No, you don't,' said Alonso.

So in the same way that I'd been talked ou[t of] renting an attic flat with an open-top *terraza*, I also talked out of my convertible white Golf. But they v[ere] right.

Whatever Alonso did, he had a clever knac[k of] making you feel forever grateful to him for pulling o[ff a] minor miracle. I hated filling in forms, especi[ally] Spanish forms, and they had this whole bureaucr[atic] system of having second-tier trainee solicitors kn[own] as *notarios* stamp everything twice before someone had to stamp everything twice. Alonso thankf[ully] managed to smooth over all the necessary procedu[res] for a *guiri* like me to be able even to buy a car on cr[edit] in Spain, as well as sort out all the insurance and [tax.] I'd brought along a wad of pesetas in cash with me [for] the deposit, but somehow Alonso managed to negot[iate] with them about the amount of down-paym[ent]

A Load of Bull

It took me a long time to become accustomed to the left-hand drive, though, and I often found myself staring at the glove-box after I'd climbed in. I'd nonchalantly spend a few minutes searching for a tape or something, then polish the passenger side of the windscreen before getting out and going round to the other side.

I'd always park the car opposite the flat, a little further up the street, outside an ugly red-brick building with the letters CCOO on the top of it, in blood-red and white. I'd always been intrigued by this place, assuming it to be a government building of sorts – but it wasn't until another General Strike (*Huelga General*) that it literally hit home in more ways than one. The twenty-four-hour stoppage that brought the country to a standstill (soon after a December *viaducto*) was eventually supported by some eight million Spanish workers, ninety-four per cent of all salaried employees. So that was almost everyone, then ... except me.

For some reason, I assumed there was no reason why the strike should include or affect me. I didn't fully understand all the complaints about the government's economic policy, anyway, and *I* wasn't complaining. So, on the morning of the strike, I innocently put on my navy-blue suit, stripey blue shirt and red tie, glued my bushy hair down, and walked out into the courtyard of my Lope de Vega flat to stroll to work. But I got punched in the face before I could make it across the road.

Not only did I get punched but I got plastered with *Huelga General* stickers all over my suit, face and *gomina*-caked hair. There was a bloody mob out there! There were literally thousands of people out in the middle of the street, all the way down to the Paseo del Prado, all waving placards and banners, with many clinging to the railings of my courtyard gates, and *even* – wait for it – *sitting on the top of my Golf!* Thank God it *wasn't* a soft-top.

It transpired that the CCOO building across the road was the HQ of the communist-led trade union federation Comisiones Obreras, and the mad mob was meeting outside my front gate before the march.

'*Esquirol! Esquirol! Esquirol!*' they started to shout, pointing directly at me as I quietly edged my way out across the courtyard and through the gates.

'Squirrel?' I thought. Why were they calling me a squirrel?

'*Esquirol! Esquirol! Esquirol!*'

'*Espera – soy inglés!* Wait, I'm English!' I shouted back – which was an utter cheek, I suppose, making a point of being foreign when it suited me. Who cared if I was *inglés*? I should *not* have been strolling to work that day in full view of the CCOO, and especially not in a suit and tie.

'*Esquirol! Esquirol! Esquirol!*'

Do I look like a squirrel?

'Who are you calling a squirrel?' I yelled, rising to

the challenge. And: 'Hey, *you*!' I added, bawling at the bearded freak on top of my Golf. 'Yes, *you*! Get off my car, you short-arsed, hairy –'

That's when I got punched.

I can't remember much else, apart from trying to sprint to safety like a novice matador who had just felt the tip of a bull's horn graze his arse for the first time. I later discovered *'esquirol'* was a 'scab' – a strike-breaker, and nothing whatsoever to do with bushy-tailed rodents who live in trees and scoff acorns. In a perverse way, I felt a sense of pride. I decided to convince myself that I'd been mistaken for a Spaniard. I had *arrived*. I had finally been accepted as one of them, albeit a scabby one.

21

My scabby metamorphosis into a working (or rather, strike-breaking) *Madrileño* started to usher in a whole new Spanish vocabulary, too, helped along by mundane, sporadic conversations with the likes of my barber, doctor – or even cleaning lady.

My cleaning lady's name was Puri, short for Purificación, meaning Purification – and about the most appropriate name for someone on a weekly mission to purify my flat.

I'd never met her and had no idea what she looked like. I didn't know her surname, where she lived, whether she was married or not, or even how old she was. Whilst she must have known a lot about me, from the state of my bathroom, duvet or boxers, I knew absolutely nothing about her. In fact, my only communication with her was in instructions left in poor Spanish back in the Lope de Vega flat.

I was told by a neighbour who also used her, that

while Puri dusted, polished, ironed and generally purified the flat every Tuesday, she would always bolt up the door from the inside, turn her portable radio on full blast and even take the phone off the hook so that nothing could disturb her.

Because Madrid was such a small world, I often wondered if I did in fact already know her. She could have been the beautiful girl I saw getting off the bus in the Paseo del Prado each morning as I strolled past on my way to work. On one occasion I thought I'd found her, when one *Madrileña* whom I was drunkenly trying to chat up turned round to me and said, 'I know more about you than you think.'

'You're not Purr-*huri*, are you?' I slurred.

'Not what?'

'You *know* ... Purification. The girl who cleans my flat ...'

The evening ended abruptly with a full glass of *Marqués de Arienzo* 1982 Rioja thrown in my face. My white shirt turned dark red, albeit with a pleasing bouquet of rounded fruit and oak.

So who *was* Puri? I continued to fantasise about what she looked like and soon found myself tidying up the flat before she arrived, trying to leave it as spotless as possible to make a good impression. *I* was cleaning it for *her*. Then I met her.

I'd even forgotten that Tuesday was a purification day when I left the office mid-morning in an urgent rush to get to Valencia, where I needed to stay a night. I'd forgotten my overnight bag and so I kept a taxi waiting while I rushed through the courtyard of Lope de Vega and up to my first-floor apartment, quickly putting the key in the lock ... only to find that it was bloody well bolted from inside.

Purification!

I didn't want to meet her and break the romantic spell that she had cast upon me, but I had no option. I could hear music playing as I started pushing the doorbell and knocking on the door, gently at first, but then harder and harder when I realised she obviously couldn't hear me. I was conscious of the taxi waiting below, so I kept my finger on the bell and started thumping on the door as hard as I possibly could, screaming out her name like some half-witted homicidal maniac with an acute Spanish speech impediment.

'*Puri! Abre la puerta! Puri!* Open the door! *Puri!*'

Finally the music stopped. I heard her unbolting the door, but then she opened it just a fraction, keeping it on the chain as she peered out.

'Who the fuck are you?' she grunted, in Spanish.

Purificación was not only rude, but not very pretty either. In fact, she looked like a hippo. This was a disaster – our relationship would never be the same again. At the very least, I'd expected more than just *one* tooth.

'*Quien coño es usted?*' she grunted again.

'I live here,' I whined. '*Vivo aqui.* I'm *Teeem Parfeee* –'
'*Quien?*'
'*Teeeeem fucking Parfeeeeeee!*'

A Load of Bull

It took me ages to convince her, eventually persuading her to at least let me into the flat and prove my identity by showing her my passport in the bedside table.

'*Ah-hah, Señor Parfeeee!*' she exclaimed, looking as relieved as me. 'You need to buy a new ironing-board cover!'

'Repeat after me,' said María Teresa, celebrating my good news of not only putting a face to Puri's name (albeit a big bloated hippo's face) but finally getting her to do some ironing, after investing in a new ironing-board cover. '*Pancha plancha con cuatro planchas. Con cuantas planchas Pancha plancha?*'

It was another one of María Teresa's tongue-twisters and it meant, 'Pancha irons with four irons. With how many irons does Pancha iron?'

It was all part of teaching me how to pronounce the letter *p* properly, which is the same as in English except that no puff of breath follows it. In fact, a piece of tissue paper hung two inches from the lips should barely move when one utters *p* in Spanish, although I decided not to stay near María Teresa's desk long enough for a demonstration.

Life in Madrid was great. It was fantastic. In fact, it was the dog's *cojones*. With my increasing involvement on *Casa Vogue*, Luis had not only been generously upping my salary, but I now had two new employees under my charge – a Guadalupe, who'd joined us as Morris was due to return to Milan, and a Sylvia de los Reyes, which meant Sylvia of the Kings. Sylvia was my own, new, young, attractive, red-haired secretary, and she was just brilliant, as not only did she understand me, she also understood my pathetic Spanish.

I realised this when my front door key broke off in the lock one day. While I was *outside*, trying to get in. Luckily I had my miniature dictionary with me, so after cursing everything in sight, I looked up the word for locksmith and, sure enough, it was utterly unpronounceable: *cerrajero*. Now, María Teresa would have first tortured me by asking me to repeat very slowly after her, *'Jorge el cerrajero vende cerrajes en la cerrajería,'* meaning, 'George the locksmith sells locks in the locksmith shop,' but *that's* why 'Sylvia of the Kings' was the best secretary in the world. I only had to phone from a call-box and tell her I needed a Sarah Hairo and she knew exactly what to do.

22

With Spain frantically gearing up for the 1992 Barcelona Olympics, the Seville Expo, and Madrid as the Cultural Capital, my career suddenly changed gear too, much to my total bewilderment.

It started one evening back at the Lope de Vega flat, while I was devouring a can of *fabada* beans. I'd been pondering the prospects of our flagging *Casa Vogue* when I suddenly thought that maybe we should print an English or bilingual version of our magazine to attract international advertising. Still the *guiri*, it would mean *I'd* be able to understand it more easily, too. On the eve of '92, Spain was being swarmed with international brands, all potential advertisers, all keen to be part of the buzz of the 'new Europe'. To my utter shock, Luis agreed to the idea.

Not only did he agree, but he decided that the 'Englishman in Madrid' attack would be ideal for seeking all the institutional support. And so *Señor*

Parfeeee unwittingly became the one wheeled out to pitch to big clients and sponsors. I didn't really know what the hell was going on but it was too late. Luis became obsessed, whilst *I* didn't even know where to start. I felt as if I was trying to glue all the crockery back together in a Pamplona china shop after the bulls had crashed through the front door and were still hurtling around. But Luis ordered an assault on every institution in Spain, starting with the national airline, Iberia.

I'm not even sure if Luis knew what he'd let himself in for by giving me the green light to relaunch *Casa Vogue* in this way, but he certainly seemed relaxed once María Teresa had organised a lunch for us at the exclusive Zalacaín, one of Madrid's premier restaurants, together with Señora Paz ('Mrs Peace') from Iberia. I started to fret before the first course even arrived. Would I be able to sip and not gulp the wine, nibble and not wolf down the food? Would they hear my guts rumbling? How long could I sit there nodding and pretending to understand everything? When should I deliver my rehearsed pitch? Would I bugger it all up? It seemed all too likely somehow.

This was my first 'selling' lunch with Luis, although you'd never have guessed he was selling anything. The choice of restaurant was an indication of how much he liked to do things in style, and it was an attitude to life that became wonderfully, if rather dangerously, contagious. To be in his company was to really witness how good life itself was. It helped that not only the setting in the three-Michelin-starred Zalacaín was luxurious, but that the Basque-based cuisine was pure luxury, too, with Luis ordering vintage wine to accompany exquisite food. I watched in awe as he did all the groundwork, charming Mrs Peace with consummate skill – softly recounting everything he could about his multicultural and widely travelled life, cleverly thrown in between discussing routes that Iberia covered across the globe. By the time he'd reintroduced me as his 'young protégé in Spain', inviting me to explain my proposal to her while apologising that we were just 'two innocent foreigners in love with her country' – an Italian-Brazilian and an *inglesito* – she was utterly taken in. I started to stammer my rehearsed Spanish, but it soon rallied itself once Luis had replenished my glass. By the time we'd dropped Mrs Peace back at her office, she'd agreed to purchase four pages in our special edition, as well as buy 5,000 copies to offer her passengers. She signed up there and then.

The next meeting I had on my own – with ONCE – was not so easy. ONCE, you see, is the Organización Nacional de Ciegos Españoles – literally meaning the 'National Organisation of Blind Spaniards' – and Sylvia, bless her, had organised a meeting for me to pitch to them.

ONCE just happens to be one of the richest groups in Spain, and their logo is instantly recognisable to any Spaniard because they sponsor numerous events. I read in John Hooper's book, *The New Spaniards*, that ONCE was created by Franco in 1938 to provide employment for the blind, whose numbers had increased during the civil war, and to organise local tax-exempt raffles to provide funding. Hooper explains that the blind man or woman at every other street corner draped with strips of lottery tickets soon became an integral part of Spanish street life. The organisation soon developed into a sophisticated welfare system for its members, creating ONCE schools and institutions for the disabled. After Franco, when ONCE began to face competition from newly legalised casinos, it launched a nationwide lottery and several 'super draws' in place of provincial draws. Before long, the blind ONCE vendors were earning almost double the average national wage, and its senior executives driven around in bullet-proof limousines – the administrators of a financial empire with huge influence.

By the time I got to see them, ONCE was worth over seventy billion pesetas (£380 million), of which half was invested in supermarket chains, tourist developments and even Tele 5, the new television channel partly owned by the media-tycoon and future Prime Minister of Italy, Silvio Berlusconi. The blind ONCE chairman, Miguel Durán, had even become Tele 5's chairman, the first time that day-to-day control of a TV station had been given to a blind man.

So ONCE was a pretty powerful group, so much so that its members and vendors would often go on strike if they didn't get their own fair share of lottery ticket commissions, though how they could tell if any *esquirols* tip-toed past their picket lines, I'm not sure.

Because ONCE was loaded, Luis had instructed me to create an extra special eight-page 'advertorial' promotion, and one morning, I duly headed off alone to their headquarters in the Calle de Prado to sell it to a Señor Garcia, head of marketing.

I should have realised that something might be up as I entered the lift and noticed that, not only were all the signs and lift-buttons *only* in Braille, but that I was actually ascending with two perfectly formed blind people. When I got out at the next floor, I headed down the corridor with my presentation folder under my arm, a few copies of *Vogue* and *Casa Vogue*, together with all our media information. Thankfully each office door had its name plaque written in both Braille and normal letters.

'*Hola,*' said Señor Garcia as I entered his office, cheerfully getting up from behind his desk and making his way towards me with one hand outstretched. I managed to guide it awkwardly into my own. His eyes were fixed on the ceiling. '*Señor Parfeee, correcto?*'

I took a moment to assess the situation. *Everything* was in Braille or uniquely adapted to his needs – the typewriter, the phone, the filing system, the lot. It was impressive. I started to unpack my presentation folder and spread several copies of *Vogue* and *Casa Vogue* across his desk, and it was then – and only then – that I suddenly really appreciated the fact that he couldn't see any of it.

Vogue is the most visual magazine in the world. But he couldn't see the wonderful eight-page promotion that we'd mocked up or the ONCE logo placed perfectly on each page, showing beautiful model couples and families enjoying art exhibitions together. I knew I couldn't adapt to the situation with my dreadful Spanish.

'Er …' I began. 'I wanted to show you – or rather – er – introduce our titles to you – you know, *Vogue* magazine and –'

'*Bo-Gay, si,*' he said, nodding cheerfully and blinking quite a bit, yet still with that fixed stare at the ceiling. '*Conozco Bo-Gay.*'

'*Conozco Bo-Gay*' meant he 'knew' about *Vogue*. He *knew* about it! But could he *see* it? No, he couldn't! He couldn't see a bloody thing!

'Well, I don't really know where to start …' I said, very honestly.

'*Claro,*' he nodded, in full appreciation of my predicament.

'You've *heard* of *Vogue*, though, then …' I continued.

'*Claro.*'

There was a pause. I decided that there was no other option: I would just have to go for it.

'That's great, then! Because we've designed a promotion to promote ONCE,' I said, pathetically. 'It's in the style of – er, the *Vogue* style of editorial pages – which is a bit like a fashion shoot, you see – no, sorry – *look* – no, sorry – but anyway, it will appear as if we're endorsing your brand and that it's *fashionable* for ONCE to be *in* Vogue – and thus, *fashionable*, too, in a sense, to be, er – to be ... to be ... *to be* –' Oh, fuck, no! – I started to panic – you can't say 'blind' as if it's an accessory! As if 'being blind' is this season's new catwalk colour. '– not *blind*,' I heard myself say. 'But, you know, fashionable to be, like, well, you know ... associated with ONCE.'

At least he couldn't see me burying my head in my hands. I wondered what the bloody hell I was doing there – an Englishman trying to flog a blind Spaniard a 40,000-quid promotion in a magazine that *I* couldn't pronounce, and *he* couldn't even sodding well see! But Señor Garcia was very understanding.

'Leave it all with me,' he said. 'It sounds most interesting.'

'Yes, of course,' I said, but then felt hideously guilty again after delivering my parting comment.

'I can see myself out.'

As the special edition of *Casa Vogue* snowballed on, Luis dispatched me off to meetings with Ana Puértolas, the editor. The first time we went somewhere, I was terrified.

I'd followed her down in the lift at Sir Rhino Twes, assuming we'd hail an air-conditioned, comfortable taxi. Instead, she unclipped a crash-helmet from her scooter. She beckoned me to sit on the back, even though she had just the one helmet. As we dodged between the traffic, I clung on for dear life, screaming at her to slow down. I looked like a senile joy-rider: a windy Englishman in a suit and tie clutching my papers under one arm, sitting upright and uptight, with my glued hair unravelling wildly and reverting to a mad, frizzy bush.

Ana and Giovanni eventually threw a cocktail-*ito* in the offices to celebrate the bumper issue, and Luis was over the moon. By the time Jonathan, our chairman, visited us again, accompanied by his uncle Si, I'd somehow also persuaded our printer to reduce their prices by twenty-five per cent. I had well and truly arrived.

As if in response to my unwelcome arrival and unexpected rise, José Manuel, the commercial director, decided to join the right-wing daily newspaper, *ABC*, founded in 1905 and a true survivor of Franco's regime. He was replaced by a José Luis in another one of Luis Carta's 'reshuffles', which also brought in our former Milan correspondent, Rachele, as editor of *Vogue*, and left me, baffled, as executive publisher for the whole group. Now when Jonathan paid us a monthly visit, I was called in to see him on three or four separate occasions to update him on the progress of each area of the business under my charge. He must have wondered, like me, what the hell was going on.

23

One day, not long after the 'reshuffle', Luis called me into his office.

'*Teeeem,*' he said. 'Do you have a *smóking?*'

'Smoking?'

'*Smóking* is a dinner-jacket,' explained María Teresa, poking her head around his door. I waited to hear what else she had to say but was alarmed to discover that she'd finished. Not only that, but Luis looked like he was also expecting a reply.

'A dinner-jacket?' I managed.

Then Giovanni arrived, flapping a sheet of paper in his hands which looked like a table-seating plan.

'Yes, *do* you have a dinner-jacket?' said Giovanni.

'No. I mean, I *used to*, I think. But not *here*. Not in Spain, surely –?'

'Buy one,' said Luis, his eyes narrowing with mischief. 'We're off to a party …'

The 'party' I then went to with Luis actually lasted

for the next four years. Not only did I *go* to the parties, I had to help organise most of them, too. I found myself enlisted into a sort of Spanish *Vogue fiesta*-planning team of myself, Luis and Giovanni. We started with a glitzy *Vogue*-Chanel fashion show and sit-down dinner within the sandy arena of Las Ventas bullring, one hot September night. Sitting on a gilt-edged chair at a candlelit table in the middle of the sand under the moon and stars was more than surreal. While doing my best to get loaded on all the Rioja, I also took several puffs of something I was discreetly offered by Francisco. Like some glorious apparition, Claudia Schiffer then suddenly emerged on the torch-lit catwalk. Watching that slinky, stilettoed figure oozing towards us in the skimpiest of Chanel outfits to the thunderous and magnificent sound of Pavarotti, I started to feel rather peculiar. To steady myself, I tried to focus on a fixed point within the rising tiers of seats circling above. It didn't help. I might just as well have been slamming endless tequilas with Manili, the monkey-faced matador, unaware that a raging *toro* was charging out towards me ...

Oh, shit. Inside the Museu Taurino – the 'Bullfighting Museum' attached to the Las Ventas arena itself – you will find such delights as the scratched, distressed bronze bust of the famous matador Juan Belmonte, with its hard-edged, protruding nose, dented chin and hollow, harrowing eyes. There's also the 'suit of lights' from probably the greatest bullfighter of all time – Manolete – bloodstained from his fatal goring in

1947. If that's not gory enough, there's also the syringe they used in vain to give him a *brazo a brazo* – an 'arm to arm' blood transfusion. And if *that's* not gory enough, then there's probably still a stain from my projectile puke of blood-red Rioja against the wall outside.

I had to be careful not to throw up at the next *Vogue fiesta* – and not just because our chairman would be present. It was going to be hosted by a chap called Joseph Zappala – who just happened to be President George Bush Senior's ambassador to Spain.

Luis had wanted to see if Zappala would be willing to throw the party to celebrate an issue of Spanish *Vogue* dedicated to the United States, so Giovanni and I had dutifully escorted him to the ambassador's residence in the Paseo de la Castellana, just behind the Embassy. When Zappala greeted us in one of the huge, chandeliered reception rooms, he'd clasped Giovanni's hand extravagantly with a 'Well, *hi* there, Giovanni! It's great to see you again!' – although it was unclear where they'd met before. Again, I wondered what the bloody hell I was doing there. It occurred to me how easy this would have been to arrange. 'Prince Giovanni, cousin of the king, would like to see the ambassador to discuss Spanish *Vogue*'s issue dedicated to the United States?' 'Why, *of course* …'

Everything went to plan, thank *Dios*. Giovanni waffled on about the Spanish royal family for a while. Luis piled on the charm and did a brilliant spiel about our special stars-and-stripes issue. Then *I* joined in, as rehearsed, to casually mention that we were looking for a suitable all-American venue in Madrid to throw a party to celebrate the issue, giving Zappala just enough time to interrupt on cue with 'Why, what the heck, let's do it here!' and feel it was his own idea all along.

'What a clever thought,' Giovanni had chirped. 'Most generous.'

I didn't throw any hughies at the eventual cocktail party, which was probably just as well, as I got stuck chatting to one of Zappala's daughters for a long time. I was unable to get away from her politely, but Jonathan Newhouse kept coming up and nudging me, asking me if I'd managed to get her number.

OK, he'd obviously noticed me leering at Miss Zappala in some kind of pathetic, crestfallen way. Maybe there *was* something wrong with me, and maybe Jonathan could see it. I'd been trying to avoid facing up to it ever since I'd split up with Chantal, but I knew what it was. My problem was that things just weren't working out with the women. I mean, it was all very well organising extravagant *fiestas* with Luis and Giovanni, and going on insane benders with Adolfo, but according to the Condé Nast chairman, I should have at least tried to get into the American ambassador's daughter's knickers. How did I fail to do that?

Talking of which, Adolfo had a long, thin red mark across his forehead the next time we met up.

'And that is?' I'd asked, pointing.

'A knicker-elastic burn,' he'd said, almost triumphantly.

I hadn't been able to take him seriously again after that.

We were now in La Dolores bar, just fifty paces from my front door. In a sense, it was all part of a new strategy. Adolfo had fathomed that the nearer to my flat (my *'piso'*) we went on a *marcha*, the more chance we'd have of coercing the *señoritas* we were with back there 'later on'. I was in a privileged position, he'd explained, because I *did* have my own *piso*. Most Spanish 'boys' my age, Adolfo included, still lived with their parents and resisted every temptation to leave the nest, with many still living there until marriage, and sometimes even *after* marriage. The family unit was far more important than any material gain in Spain, so much so that moving away from comfort and security was regarded as a failure rather than an achievement. And most Spanish mothers couldn't understand why their sons should *ever* want to leave home. Even after marriage, it should be the wife who was expected to move away from *her* family, not him.

It wasn't always such a rosy picture of family bliss, though. A recent report in *El País* newspaper detailed the case of a 44-year-old Spaniard who was finally being evicted from his parents' house, as well as being sued for over twenty years of unpaid rent. *He*, meanwhile, was counter-suing his parents for failing to make payments towards his upkeep.

Anyway, there we all were in La Dolores bar – I say

'all', because somehow, an hour or so ago, Adolfo had also managed to pick up two *señoritas* along the way, having spotted and moved in on them as snappily as a flamenco tap step. Adolfo had quickly attached himself to the one called Desideria, which I thought meant 'Desire', so *he'd* be OK. Her friend was Leya – 'Loyal'. 'Loyal' lived up to her name from the outset by making it clear that she had a very steady boyfriend back home in Málaga. She was a lost cause. I was tired, hungry and already tipsy, but I still tagged along for the ride.

Leya had corkscrew red hair, jangled with no end of bracelets and bangles, and wore suede cowboy boots with tassels. She explained that not only was she from Málaga, but that she was a *boqueron*. Now, being a *boqueron* can mean many things. It can mean that you are a little sardine, or a loud-mouth, or even a loud-mouthed little sardine. It can also mean that you are an *authentic* person – and that's what Leya was: an authentic *boqueron* from Málaga. This meant she would die to save the things from Málaga, its people, its streets, its customs, its Easter parade, not to mention her Málaga boyfriend, who was no doubt also a loud-mouthed, hairy little *boqueron* as well. She had no interest in Madrid where she was reluctantly visiting her friend, 'Desire', and certainly no interest in England, *or* me. In fact, I was beginning to realise that Spanish women didn't really need me at all. And I still don't think they'd really forgiven me for the defeat of the Armada in 1588, either. But once we'd firmly established all that, Leya and I got on marvellously. I just had to pretend that I was interested in hearing about Málaga all night, whilst watching Adolfo tongue Desideria out the corner of my eye.

As the night drew on, we moved further and further up the Calle de Huertas and away from my *piso* – much to Adolfo's frustration. Because Leya and I had no intention of glueing our mouths together, we picked at garlicky *tapas* and even shared a dish of diced chunks of fishy-smelling squid soaking in their own Málaga black ink. While Leya and I then charmed one another through black-stained, garlic teeth, Adolfo and Desideria picked at aphrodisiac anchovies and oysters.

It was all very well Adolfo plotting for the *señoritas* to come back to my *piso* 'later on' – but how much bloody *later on* could it possibly be? It was already three in the morning yet again. I'd finally sussed that this was just *typical* of Spanish girls – stringing you along until dawn when you were too pissed and knackered to try it on anyway. Spaniards never hurried to finish anything, and the fact that most appointments were never adhered to was *etiquette*. They considered it rude to leave the company of someone before they'd told them absolutely everything they wanted to tell them. As it was also rude to interrupt, the Spaniards they were talking to never let on that they had other appointments, either – relaxed, no doubt, in the fact that whoever they were going on to meet would *also* be an hour or so late.

By four in the morning I was out of my skull again. We'd ended up in the Villa Rosa *tablao*-style nightclub, off the Plaza de Santa Ana, with all its ornate-tile décor – one of those 'so-kitsch-it's-chic' venues where flamenco meets rock. Adolfo was dancing like a psycho again, sort of *limboing* up towards poor Desideria, crouching low and stretching back while spreading his legs and arms apart, as if he was about to rugby-tackle her. Soon, no doubt, he would get his nipples out. Worryingly, 'Miss Loyal' seemed to suddenly forget all her inhibitions, too. As I slurred at her over the loud music, she started jiving wildly and clapping her hands above her head, beckoning me to do the same. I *couldn't*. The flashing strobes kept catching everyone's white teeth – except hers. The squid ink had stained them so black it looked as if someone had punched them out. As I moved away and caught sight of myself in the mirror behind the bar, I realised I looked the same.

Near the bar, talking to friends and minding his own business, was the film director, Pedro Almodóvar. I was very drunk but he also looked as if he'd had a few. He was a chubby, funny-looking chap. I was about to go up to him to recount my idea for a movie about a kidnapped matador, but he caught my eye and looked like he was silently pleading with me not to. I swayed back to my *piso* instead and passed out, oblivious to the front-door buzzer going an hour or so later when Adolfo had finally steered 'Desire' and 'Loyal' back to mine for a 'nightcap'. 'Loyal', he later told me, was raring to be disloyal. I'd missed out on another opportunity.

24

I was exhausted. As both the *marcha* and *fiestas* increased, so did the tasks that Luis kept sending me on. In fact I'd just flown from Madrid to Vienna, then Barcelona, then hired a car to Valencia, then flown back to Madrid and on to Paris, then back to Madrid again – all within a few days. I was thirty-one but much of the time felt very near to death. I was convinced I was on the verge of a heart attack, or as Doctor Broschi called it in his very soft, soothing voice, an *infarto*.

'A what?'

'*Infarto.* Heart attack – but don't worry,' he said, feeling my pulse, and almost whispering as he spoke, 'you're not having a heart attack.'

I had come to see Dr Broschi at the bilingual Unidad Médica practice, convinced of my nervous exhaustion, as well as the fact that I was always shaky and that my stomach was constantly rumbling.

'Your stomach rumbles?' he said.

'Yes – do you think it could be a tumour?'

'No.'

'Oh.'

'When does it rumble?'

'All the bloody time.'

'Can you not be more precise?'

'In the mornings ... then, er, most of the afternoons.'

'Is it wind?' he asked, straight to the point.

This was very embarrassing.

'Well, yes, I suppose it is. Yes. Yes, that's what it could be. A touch of wind.'

'And do you expel it?'

'Do I what?'

'Expel it.'

Oh, for crying out loud! Did we have to discuss all this? He was waiting patiently for a reply.

'Yes, Dr Broschi,' I managed at last. 'I expel it. Sometimes. Yes.'

He stared at me. We both knew what his next question was going to be and I think we were both dreading it. Finally it came:

'Burps or farts?'

Sensing my predicament, he kindly tried to ask it in a different tone to lighten my embarrassment.

'Burps or *farts?*' he repeated louder, as if asking me if I'd like tea or coffee. Then he said it in Spanish, too:

'Eructos o pedos?'

'Eructos,' I said, if only to stop him. 'Burps.'

'No farts?'

'No.'

'No farts at all?'

'Not really, no.'

'*Never* any farts?' he persisted, somewhat suspiciously.

I took a deep breath.

'Sometimes farts, yes,' I relented, grinning awkwardly.

But he didn't need to know it was ninety-nine per cent farts. It wasn't any of his business that I'd spent half my time in Madrid to date as an uptight Englishman, trying desperately to hold my farts *in*, and then the other half secretly farting my way around all the beautiful streets and parks in Madrid.

Nor did he need to know about my other little problem – the fact that I couldn't even take a crap at work. Not at *Vogue España!* It wasn't really a medical problem. It had something to do with the layout of the office and the fact that the gents looked out towards the interior patio and directly across to María Teresa's desk the other side of the reception area, shielded only by a large window with frosted glass. How could anyone relax under such conditions? I kept worrying that if I spent too long in there, María Teresa herself would start tapping on the frosted glass, reciting another tongue-twister for me to repeat, like, 'How many sheets could a sheet slitter slit if a sheet slitter could slit sheets?'

So Dr Broschi did *not* need to know that I often

trotted urgently up to the parallel Calle de Velázquez, and then darted desperately into the five-star toilets at the Hotel Wellington instead, or even sometimes, on a very bad day, that I'd march all the way back to my *piso* in Lope de Vega. He wouldn't understand what I had to endure living here as an Englishman.

'So you have no problem expelling it?' continued Dr Broschi.

'No, not really,' I said, mortified with embarrassment.

Ten minutes later and he'd weighed me, measured me, asked me to take my shirt off and lie flat on the couch, then prodded and squeezed my belly and listened to all the rumbling through his stethoscope.

'There's no doubt about it,' he said. 'That's one hell of a lot of wind.'

'Is it?'

'Yes, it is. You're suffering from incarcerated flatulence.'

So it *was* a sort of *in-fart-o* after all ...

According to Dr Broschi, all my problems came down to trapped wind – while all along I thought I'd been expelling quite enough of it already. But, no, he wanted me to expel more. He wanted me to fart my brains out! He also wanted me to eat and drink less to lose a stone or two, try to get to bed before four in the morning once in a while, as well as cut back on all the coffee that Sylvia kept pouring me – because *that's* what was making me shaky, he believed.

By the end of the month, I'd been put through a

complete medical and physical examination, even sprinting away furiously on a machine with the whole cardiograph thing wired up to my chest. But although Dr Broschi had experimented on me with tablets to change my stomach's 'flora lining', being English meant being bottled up. And being bottled up meant trapped wind. It was a fact of life.

And work wasn't about to get any easier. Everything had suddenly become all very Euro-friendly, with 'pan-European' strategies being a priority for every business one encountered, including Condé Nast.

I'd been sent to Vienna, for example, because Luis decided that Spain – or rather, I – should get involved with an annual conference on the worldwide distribution of magazines. So I attended our pre-conference, pan-European Condé Nast seminar, but it was just an excuse for another gastronomic piss-up. I started to wonder how our beetroot-faced distribution controller, another José Luis, was going to understand any of what I told him when I reported back on the latest distribution methods.

'Look, José,' I could hear myself say. 'We're going to start a Spanish *Vogue* subscribers' club in Bangladesh. Wha'd'ya think of that?'

'*Joder!*' he'd reply, which in Spanish can mean, 'Fuck me!' or 'Why don't you just fuck off back to your own country and leave us in peace, you fat English git?'

'Well done, José,' I would have to say. 'Jolly good. Let's do that, then.'

And then Luis had sent me to Paris for yet another

pan-European Condé Nast get-together to see if there was any cost saving in us all buying the paper we printed our magazines on together. There wasn't. You try telling the editor of French *Vogue* that she had to use the same paper as Spain, and you might just as well tell her that you'd shat yourself in her brand new Prada handbag. We weren't ready to be a Europe at all, not when it came to *Vogue*.

What I'm trying to explain is how chaotic my life had become. Whatever happened to those simple six weeks in Madrid to help out on the launch? I needed a *life*. I needed sun and *bougainvillaea* ... that cobbled, whitewashed, pool-side Spain. Most of all, I still needed a *señorita*.

25

Whilst my Spanish was slowly improving, my chat-up lines were still atrocious and I'd realised that stalking *Madrileñas* with Adolfo was futile. So instead, I wondered if I might be able to find the female equivalent of *me* – a foreigner living in Madrid who was also lonely and dying for it. Driven by lust, I went along to a God-awful British Chamber of Commerce lunch, held in the Hotel Inter-Continental. I then spent the next five years trying to avoid ever going again. There were no women and the average age was eighty.

I then decided I would hang out at a riding school. I could picture myself trotting towards a Penélope Cruz-like figure, as she shook her hair loose and leant against the stable door in her tight jodhpurs and white blouse, showing just a hint of Iberian nipple whilst sexily tapping a riding crop against her boot. The whole country-club culture was a complex one in Madrid, though, with membership of the very exclusive and extortionate Club de Campo or Puerta de Hierro being virtually impossible for foreigners. So I joined an unstuffy little riding club called the *Club Equitación de Somosaguas*.

Although the club was pleasantly shabby, I soon discovered that they took their riding very seriously. Too seriously. They were more accustomed to nurturing Spanish Olympic show-jumpers than prats like me, who just wanted to gallop through the adjacent Casa de Campo looking for jodhpur-totty. Before being allowed to gallop off in search of Penélope Cruz, I was forced to participate in humiliating classes with a bunch of eight-year-old pony-club girls. The Spanish horse vocabulary didn't come easily, either – and with all the shouting, panting and the sound of hooves pounding the hard sand, I could never make out whether the instructor, Raphael, wanted me to stop, go, trot, walk, rise, fall, shorten or lengthen the rein, or maybe just bugger off home altogether.

So I stuck to tennis and swimming at the club and when I felt the need to venture further out of Madrid, I drove off to the Navacerrada mountains, taking the off-season chair-lift to the peak to enjoy the views before trekking all the way back down for lunch – alone and free. One of my favourite café bars in the whole of Spain became the El Abeto in the centre of the Alpine-looking village of Navacerrada itself, at the foot of the mountain. It was a semi-circular sun-trap, facing the fountain in the little cobblestone *plaza*. I could sit there for hours on one of their director-chairs or on the wooden bench against the timber and stone construction, with the smell of the pines and the log fires, reading what bits I could understand in a Spanish newspaper, or just watching the people stroll by – weekend *Madrileño* skiers in winter but locals, too – savouring aperitifs before a late, long lunch at somewhere like the Casa Felipe Asador. I felt happier and healthier than I'd felt for some time ... and my diabolical serpent suddenly bucked up, too.

Donna and Samantha were two blondes on holiday from San Diego. They were on a European hen tour before one of them got married back in sunny California, and were the daughters of friends of friends of Luis. He'd slyly told me they were *'guapas'* and had somehow passed on my number. They eventually called to ask if I knew of a really cheap hotel in Madrid where they might stay for the week ahead.

I was immediately on the phone to Adolfo, and a plan was concocted. I was to book them into the seediest *hostal* we could find, just off the Gran Vía, to see how long it took them to come begging to stay at Lope de Vega.

It took less than an hour.

'Hi, Tim,' said the pretty Californian voice from the call-box when Sylvia put the call through to me on the Monday morning. 'It's Samantha –'

'*Samantha?*' I hesitated. 'Oh, *that* Samantha. Hi, how's it going?'

'It's going bad. There's no *way* we can stay here. It – is – *so* – dirty.'

I was glowing.

I picked them up in the Golf and charmed them with *tapas* at the Espejo. The intention was for Donna and Samantha to share the double bed in my room, and for me to graciously move into the spare bedroom like a true gentleman – but bollocks to that. I left them alone on Monday with a spare key and various guidebooks, and by the time I'd rejoined them after work, they were ready for a night out on the town.

Unlike those exhausting, serpent-teasing *Madrileñas*, however, these Californian girls didn't need to be entertained with a *marcha* until four in the morning. By midnight, after a boozy, provocative dinner with Adolfo followed by a tour of just one terrace bar, they suggested we head back to the *piso*, where *they* then also decided we should play strip spin-the-bottle. Adolfo was delirious. Each time the girls lost, they swiftly manoeuvred themselves into a state of undress as skilfully as a pair of synchronised-swimmers. I ended up where I belonged – in my own room with the raunchy Samantha – the one who *wasn't* getting married. I wish I could pretend it was like something out of one of those erotica books – you know, *the trickle of retreating silk, the elasticity of her rhythmic hands, first kneading, then lightly teasing* – but it was nothing like that at all. I eventually passed out while she had her frenzied, furious way with me, like some nympho trapeze-artist let loose in an all-night amusement park. I kept suddenly bolting upright, wide-awake to discover her still having rides on anything she could find that would still let her on. That night I dreamt my *cojones* were being used as castanets.

When I returned to the flat the following evening, it not only looked spotless but Donna and Samantha were actually cooking for me. Adolfo arrived again and got the flamenco music going, pirouetting like a rabid matador with my corked *banderillas* above his head. As the evening took a similar wild course to the night before, I wondered whether I would ever witness such open-armed hospitality with any *Madrileña*.

In fact, it dawned on me that it had been Luis, not Adolfo, who'd sent Samantha my way, together with an injection of renewed self-confidence. By now, although I understood everything I read and most of what I heard in Spanish, *still* no one ever really understood anything when I *spoke* the bloody language. So my chances of chatting up a non-English-speaking Spanish girl still seemed slim. I would just have to use other tactics. I already had the car, the job, the plastered hair. But I still needed that ultimate *Madrileña* babe-magnet: an attic flat with a gigantic sun terrace.

26

I finally found the hottest *'ático con terraza'* I could find and took the plunge, moving out of the cool, interior Lope de Vega flat and into a convertible, roof-down shag-pad, which even had its own swimming-pool. And to avoid being talked out of it all, I didn't tell María Teresa.

The address was at the other end of Serrano, at 145 – *ciento cuarenta y cinco* – or rather, 'Sir Rhino thiento-cwawentee-thinko', next door to the Mayte Commodore, which was an old establishment luncheon club usually packed with hundreds of gold-rinsed yapping Spanish grannies.

The flat itself had more *exterior* than *interior* living space. Instead of having a proper kitchen, I had a glorious terrace – with wonderful views overlooking some of the most elegant residential mansions in the wealthy *barrio* of Madrid known as El Viso. I was next door to both the Thailand and Philippine embassies –

on the corner of Serrano with the Calle del Guadalquivir – and to my left, I had views over the roof-tops towards the white Torre Picasso tower, Madrid's solitary and modest 'executive' skyscraper, which slowly became floodlit at night, gently illuminating to form a white beacon across the city.

My new bathroom was also much smaller than at Lope de Vega, so there was no room for all those kitsch Spanish souvenirs either, which was fine by me.

I tried to get plants to grow on the *terraza* but it was impossible. I bought ivy to climb up the reinforced glass fence, but the fence acted as a magnifying glass and ended up burning it. Optimistically I bought *two* sun-beds, too, just on the off-chance of squeezing into the Federation of Sexology's statistics for outdoor *siesta*-shagging.

But not only was there no proper kitchen, there was no washing-machine or dishwasher, either. I didn't think about any of that when I first viewed the flat, but I soon realised just how good I'd had it back at Lope de Vega. I now had to wash my clothes in the bath. What I had really done was move into – or rather, onto – a *roof*, not a flat.

Opposite my patch of roof were some handy little shops that included the apparently harmless but potentially hazardous *huevería* and *lechería* – which officially sold eggs and milk, respectively.

A *huevería* egg-shop, for example, emanated from the depths of my throat as a 'web-uh-where-wia', which is nonsensical in Spanish because (as we know) there's no such thing as the letter *w*, let alone a 'web-uh-where-wia'. And eggs – or *huevos* – or rather 'web-bos', as I called them, *also* meant 'bollocks' in Spanish, just like *cojones*. Not that it followed that a *huevería* was a bollocks shop – but if you exclaim *'Huevos!'* at the right time in the right tone and at the right person, then sure enough, it means 'Bollocks!' So it wasn't easy for me (or shopkeepers) to keep a straight face when I asked for webbos, or even the creature that laid them – a *pollo* – which, if pronounced incorrectly with an 'a' instead of an 'o', meant 'prick' and not 'chicken'. I can't tell you how many odd looks I received over the years asking for half-a-dozen bollocks and boneless prick fillets.

Then there was the *lechería* milk-shop and the whole *leche* thing itself, which as far as I knew, meant milk and *only* milk. But, *oh, no…*

Along came a nutcase called Señor Ruíz-Mateos, an entrepreneur who fell into disgrace when his empire was expropriated by the government, and he decided to have a public punch-up with the finance minister, a Señor Miguel Boyer, whom he slapped around the head, screaming, *'Que te pego, leche!'*

Now, I thought that was a silly thing to scream, because it translated literally to 'How I hit you, milk!', but according to Sylvia, it was very rude indeed. It soon became the catchphrase of the year, although it was a long time before anyone had the courage to explain to me what it meant, and I think they only did so to stop me from continually repeating the phrase myself. *Leche*, in this context, you see, (i.e., whilst being slapped around the head) meant 'sperm'. So, '*Que te pego, leche!*' really meant 'How I hit you, you spunkhead, you!'

When not used to describe milk or spunk, *leche* had several other meanings, too, which made it quite a treacherous word to use. '*Tuve que ir cagando leches para no llegar tarde,*' for example, meant 'I had to shift my fucking arse to get there on time.' Or '*Tiene muy mala leche,*' meant, 'He's a real shit.' In fact, I soon learnt that many Spanish swear words had double-meanings, one of which was *not* a swear word, which was a nightmare for your average *guiri*.

A *chorizo*, for example, meant a hard pork sausage of some sort, but it also meant someone was a 'bloody crook', while *chulo* could mean a 'bargain', but *also* a 'cocky bugger'. And you had to be careful if someone asked you how your mum was. '*Mamá esta muy bien,*' would cheerfully mean, 'Mum's very well, thanks.' But, '*La mama muy bien,*' would mean 'She gives terrific blowjobs.'

I enjoyed swearing in Spanish, though. I liked using the word *gilipollas*, pronounced 'hilly-poyas', which meant 'silly plonker' or 'dickhead' depending on how forcefully you said it. In fact, everything depended on how forcefully you said it. Despite the verb *joder* officially meaning 'to fuck', it could also mean you were simply surprised or pissed off about something and was thus widely used in everyday speech and barely considered to be that rude at all. It was very normal to hear it uttered by politicians, businessman and within most Spanish families, simply as an emphasis or an interjection, and not as an insult at all. So because there was no literal translation for 'fuck off' in Spanish, one often had to rely on a forcefully stressed culinary combination of milk, eggs, salamis and *cojones* to tell someone where to get off. Addressing someone as an *hijo de puta* normally did the trick, too – it literally translated to 'son of a whore'.

Personally, I had to be very careful with *coño*, which meant 'cunt', because the cruel thing (and, for me, a major problem) was that it didn't *always* mean cunt, as again it depended on the way it was pronounced. '*Está en el quinto coño*,' literally translated to, 'It's in the fifth cunt.' But it didn't really *mean* that. It meant, 'It's in the middle of nowhere,' which I suppose 'it' would be if it was in the fifth cunt along ... And likewise, *'que coño!'* meant, 'what the hell!?' or 'what a pity!' and *not* 'what a cunt!' But while, *'Eres un coño'* (they're masculine, oddly) would definitely mean 'You are a cunt', *coño* on its own, thrown casually into the middle of a sentence like a sigh (a bit like *joder*) often meant nothing more than 'damn it' – although *I* could never get my *coños* to sound like sighs.

From my new attic flat, instead of pacing around the Prado, I could now take up jogging again down the quiet, leafy lanes of El Viso itself, where all the expensive houses were protected by walls and high gates, with every other doorway boasting a security alarm or a 'Beware of the dog' sign. Only the sound of children splashing in swimming pools provided evidence of human habitation, in a neighbourhood which seemed sunk in a permanent *siesta*. All the way along Guadalquivir I'd jog, down to Paseo de la Habana and along to the Plaza Sagrados Corazones, where the gigantic Bernabéu stadium of Real Madrid hugged the corner of Concha Espina with the Castellana.

From my *terraza*, if I stood on tip-toe, I could just make out the glow of floodlights and hear the faint roars of the crowd if the Bernabéu was packed. I'd been inside when Real Madrid played Barcelona and the atmosphere was electric. If they were ahead, I loved the way the crowd roared *'Olé!'* every time the home team touched the ball, which even beat Manili's antics with his matador cape. I'd been inside with 96,000 others and I was always amazed at how *civilized* they all were on leaving the stadium afterwards – although I always imagined them glancing warily in my direction, as if *I* was the one who was going to start the riot.

You see, the whole *fútbol* thing was not easy for an Englishman in Madrid. Memories of Heysel were still engraved on everyone's minds, and English clubs had only just been invited back to play in Europe. And it wasn't easy living in Madrid during the 1990 World Cup, when Spain were knocked out by Yugoslavia on the same night England scraped through against Belgium. It was very quiet in the office the next morning, although they recovered a few days later once England lost their penalty shoot-out against Germany.

But my biggest problem when it came to *fútbol* was that I was … English. Every Spaniard in the office had the same abhorrent image after assembling the words 'Englishman' and 'football' together. It was irrelevant that I was dressed in a suit and tie. Underneath it all, as far as every Spanish *fútbol* fan was concerned, I was wearing a sleeveless Union Jack vest revealing grotesque tattoos across my colossal beer-belly and a pair of sick-stained shorts. 'I went to see Real Madrid play,' I'd innocently remark, only to be met with, 'You're a *gamberro.*' This was Spanish for hooligan, and a relatively new word in their dictionary (in the old days I would have been a *rufián*). I'd explain that I sat quietly in the family enclosure and didn't drink any alcohol, but it all fell on deaf ears. I was still a *gamberro*.

Without fail, whenever I mentioned *fútbol*, the Spanish immediately assumed I spent my weekends on the rampage in Rotterdam, or fought baton-wielding Belgian riot cops and set fire to cross-channel ferries. My behaviour was intolerable – I shouldn't have been allowed to even travel abroad, let alone live within a mile of the Bernabéu. I was obviously using an alias to work at Spanish *Vogue* during the week in order to commit mindless thuggery every weekend.

27

As my involvement on *Vogue* increased, so did the *fiestas*. María Teresa kept handing me invitations to events that Luis couldn't face going to, but which I could never resist. I even got involved on *Vogue Hombre*, too – the men's magazine we banded to *Vogue*. I had to write some 'style' articles for it with predictably English topics, like tweed jackets and brogues. I wasn't sure if they understood what I wrote, as it was all about being sick over some brogues and having to pick dried vomit from the little holes, but they published it anyway.

Escorting Luis to mammoth lunchtime feasts with clients continued, too, with Alonso always driving us, even if the restaurant was less than a hundred metres from the office, as was the case for Club 31 in Alcalá. It was one of Madrid's old-fashioned establishment restaurants. With all the bossy, starched, unsmiling, uniformed waiters, all short and Franco-looking *à la* Alonso himself, and with all the dark mahogany décor and ancient Spanish maps, this restaurant was an example of Spain's clever ability to retain the best of the old regime behind heavily draped doors – in contrast, but also in parallel, to 'new Spain' outside.

It was at Club 31 where Luis and I lunched with a studious little chap called Alvaro from the Spanish Tourist Board. They wanted to do something 'seriously big' with us to celebrate 1992. Alvaro's boss was the Minister for Tourism, whose budget – judging by Spain's obsession with looking after its main revenue stream in the economy – was huge.

'We were thinking you might be able to dedicate a special magazine to Spain,' said Alvaro, once we'd plied him with the very best red wine and cuisine that Club 31 could offer. 'A sort of *Condé Nast Traveller* but dedicated entirely to our country – maybe in several other languages, too – English, German, French and Italian, possibly Japanese – banded to all your *Vogues* in the world – with an introduction by the king. Something we can use to promote a new image for Spain worldwide, for a better class of tourist.'

Luis nearly choked on his medium-rare fillet steak. I'd been obsessed with the potential of bilingual projects dedicated to Spain for ages, and little Alvaro hadn't let me down.

'Alvaro,' said Luis, refilling his glass. 'Something like that would cost –'

'We'd obviously spend what it takes –' interrupted Alvaro.

'– but we'd be talking about a figure of some six million dollars ...' said Luis.

There was a pause as Alvaro fiddled pleasurably with his wine. 'We could find over half of that,' he said finally. 'We'd find the rest through our partners – the airlines, the railways, the food and wine boards ...'

I kicked Luis under the table. I wanted to wrap it up and get out of there – and an hour or so later, we did get out, glowing brightly. Condé Nast Spain stood to make a killing. But then along came Jonathan, still living in Paris and thus heavily swayed by what the directors of French Condé Nast thought, who weren't exactly happy that Spain, at that moment in time, was seen to be more 'in *vogue*' than, say, France. Our project was threatening to jeopardise French *Vogue*'s own Seville supplement which was counting on the support from 'Turespaña', the Spanish Tourist Board. The French got to work and pretty soon Jonathan refused permission for us to proceed.

'He doesn't understand,' said Luis, throwing down the phone, having tried in vain to call Jonathan and plead our case. I'd never seen Luis so angry, but it was an odd sort of anger. He just went very quiet, almost sulking. I offered to leave the room but he waved at me to sit still. Then María Teresa came in with a fax from *Turespaña*. They'd already been told that we couldn't commit to the project and now informed us by return that they found us unprofessional and would halt all advertising in our group for the foreseeable future. Luis slammed his fist on the marble table and asked her to fax the letter through to Jonathan. He then got up, patted me on the shoulder, and told me to follow him. We left his office and headed for the front door, speaking to no-one along the way, then took the rattling old lift down to the ground floor. I didn't dare ask where we were going and nor did Alonso, shuffling nervously at the main entrance on seeing his boss because he didn't have the Jag ready to take us anywhere. Luis waved him away and guided me across Serrano to the delicatessen, Mallorca, where there was a *bodega* downstairs with a few stalls at the bar. In silence, he guided me onto one stall and eased his large frame onto the one beside me. He tugged off his tie and beckoned over the waiter, ordering two flutes of champagne. It wasn't even noon, but Luis downed his in one and urged me to do the same. The waiter refilled our glasses – and it was only on the second, slower sip, that Luis finally turned to me and raised his glass.

'To Madrid,' he said. '*Un día me matará.* One day it'll kill me …'

I appreciated more about the Spanish Tourist Board's mission to promote a new image for Spain worldwide – 'for a better class of tourist,' as Alvaro had put it – when I met my new friend, Ed.

Edward Owen was a big, bear-like character – the foreign correspondent in Spain for *Express Newspapers*. He was also the correspondent for *The Times* while at the same time freelancing for *Time-Life*, the BBC, Australian Broadcasting, NBC and Radio France Internationale, so one day he might be covering politics and boring EEC stuff, and the next chasing crooks and lager-louts on the Costa del Sol. Ed was also credited for saving the donkey, Blackie Star, named after the tabloid newspaper he also represented. It started when the 'Association for the Defence of Animal Rights' claimed that Blackie would be 'tortured as usual' at the annual Pero Palo *fiesta* of Villanueva de la Vera. 'Allegedly', a donkey is dragged through the streets with the fattest villager on top, then hit with sticks and stones before being 'crushed to death by the inebriated crowd.' The *fiesta* commemorates the arrest and hanging of a bandit called Pero Palo: centuries ago, *he* was dragged around the medieval village on a donkey, and *he* was hit before being hung. 'The donkey has suffered abuse in the past,' said Ed, 'but has never actually died.'

On the day of the *fiesta*, the ritual went ahead but afterwards the owner of the donkey was located. In a battle to save Blackie before the *Sun* did, Ed managed to buy the donkey and photographed the owner handing over a receipt. 'Gotcha!' screamed the *Star's* eventual headline, as Blackie went into quarantine prior to being shipped to a sanctuary, all paid for by the *Star's* readers.

And so it was Ed, too, who finally put me straight on goats. He explained that each year, in January, in a northern town called Manganeses de la Polvorosa – to celebrate the festival of San Vincente de Martir, the town's patron saint – locals would throw a live goat from the church belfry onto an outstretched tarpaulin, fifty feet below. The catapulted goat normally landed with legs splayed, then emerged shaken but relatively unscathed, before scampering away to become the guest of honour at the raucous *fiesta* that followed. The origins of the ritual were unclear, but according to one legend, a priest's goat, whose milk fed the poor, accidentally fell from the bell-tower and was saved by villagers holding a blanket. So I was living in a country that threw goats for fun. Great.

'Don't be alarmed,' said Ed. 'This coming year they've banned the toss. They'll be lowering the goat on ropes instead. They have to, what with it being 1992 and all that. All eyes are on Spain. So it won't be called goat throwing any more. It'll be goat *lowering* …'

Everything was improving as we were ushered into 1992. I later learned that the throwing was indeed forbidden that year and instead, the goat had to be let down on ropes. But in 1996 the ban was lifted and a goat was thrown down again. The Mayor defended his decision by stating, 'A *fiesta* without throwing a goat is like Christmas without a Christmas tree.'

28

At last, it was 1992. It was the peak of the Spanish eighties, really, the pinnacle of the post-Franco boom – as they'd been celebrating this date for the last decade. Seville had the World Fair, Barcelona the Olympics, Madrid the European Capital of Culture, while numerous events throughout Spain were scheduled to mark the five-hundredth anniversary of Columbus's voyage to America. Oh – and goats were being *lowered*, not tossed.

It's difficult to overestimate how important this '1992' was to *all* Spaniards, to the whole Spanish national psyche. The country that was isolated for over thirty years under Franco used to look for any excuse to celebrate – so much so that even winning the Eurovision Song Contest in 1968 was a big deal. So 1992 was going to be massively important. Not that it meant getting things done on time. When the World Fair started in April, King Juan Carlos arrived as the decorators left through a side-door, leaving wet paint everywhere.

Early in 1992, Tara – Tarané Tahbaz – joined us at Condé Nast Spain. Tara was Persian and according to Giovanni, her pedigree was so good that she'd be a 'Persian princess' if Persia was still Persia. But I wouldn't know anything about all that. I'd seen Tara in the offices before, even sitting in with Luis for what I presumed to be an interview, but it was Giovanni who finally introduced us, bringing her into my office and bristling with Giovanni-*esque* excitement.

'Timothy, this is Tara!' he declared. 'Tara, this is *Monsieur Parfait.*'

I couldn't work out her age, but she wasn't old and she wasn't young. She had long, jet-black hair with a white streak in the fringe like Anne Bancroft in *The Graduate*. She had big brown eyes, freckly tanned skin, and a great throaty laugh. And *as* she laughed, she kept sweeping and shaking her hair back. She was great fun. She spoke perfect English but I quickly gathered she spoke every other language as well, just like Giovanni. She wasn't tall, but she had a sexy tight figure and bum – and she was wearing jeans and a black, skintight top, highlighting her tits.

As we shook hands rather hesitantly, then went for an immediate kiss on both cheeks instead, Giovanni added, 'Yes ... Luis thought it would be jolly good if you met.'

Then Giovanni left Tara and me together – *and*, I think, somewhat both confused, although my own confusion was short-lived. I soon realised why Luis thought it would be a good idea that we should meet – and it was not only because he'd been slyly trying to set me up with someone, *anyone*, recently. In addition to Tara's good looks and taste, you see, she had an immense address book which she hadn't ever exploited, and which Luis wanted me to tap into.

I offered Tara a seat, as Sylvia brought coffee whilst eyeing me suspiciously. I started with something inane like, 'So, what brings you from Persia to Madrid?' and I was hoping for a simple reply, like, 'By flying carpet,' or something. Instead, I got her life-story. It turned out she originated from the Persian 'Afshar dynasty', and that her great, great, great-whatever was actually Nader Afshar, or King Nader, who ruled Persia from 1736 to 1747, or, 'for a couple of seasons', as Tara put it, and who was often referred to as the 'Napoleon of Iran'.

'But don't worry,' she said. 'I only inherited my temper from him.'

As it transpired that King Nader once blinded his own son merely through suspicion, then quickly regretted it and went into a tantrum, executing fifty noblemen whom he thought should have offered to be blinded instead, I decided to avoid witnessing Tara in a temper. Obviously the chap was a nutter, but he was also the greatest of all Persian rulers, winning numerous battles and even invading India to snatch the legendary 'Koh-i-Noor' diamond which Queen Victoria later incorporated in the crown jewels, and which was set as the centre-piece of the State Crown for the coronation of Elizabeth the Second.

Before long, Tara had joined the company as *Casa Vogue*'s freelance *Asesora de Decoración*, which meant that she helped find houses and people to profile, while we tapped into her contacts to get new business. She was a female Giovanni, I suppose, and going to meetings with Tara started to open up a completely new social life for me in Madrid.

On one occasion, she invited me to a pasta lunch that she was organising at her home in the very exclusive Moraleja, one of the more idyllic, luxurious and extortionate districts outside central Madrid. The many haughty guests included Giovanni and another aristocratic chap called Fernando Falcó, the 'Marqués de Cubas'. Now, old Fernando was one of the most famous blokes in Spain, but famous more than anything because his ex-wife was Marta Chávarri, the one whose satanic cauldron was snapped for posterity in a nightclub. Marta then separated from Fernando and hooked up with Alberto Cortina, one of the detective-raincoat jet-setter 'Albertos', who was then divorced from his marchioness wife, the mega-rich Alicia Koplowitz. Alicia's sister, Esther, also mega-rich, then ended up marrying Fernando. Trying to unravel the sexual exploits of *Madrileño* high society was hard going. Anyway, Fernando was the famous bloke whose wife was caught with her pants off ... but to Tara, he was a good friend. And *I* found that funny. In fact, old Fernando was also once linked with Ava Gardner.

What *was* it with Ava Gardner – and that other one, too, Rita Hayworth – with all those Spanish men?

So, Fernando and Giovanni made a big show of spinning the pasta together – and Tara kept flirting and refilling my glass in the garden, where some fifteen other lofty guests were gathered, some of whom I recognised from *¡Hola!* but couldn't put a name to. And what I'm saying is that I just *knew* Tara was trying to get me out and about into other circles, and on Luis's instructions, too, because I *also* knew he was convinced there was so much business we hadn't even scratched the surface of yet.

I soon decided that trying it on with Tara was beyond me. She would typically take me to meetings in her little car wearing a purple mini-skirt and stilettos, and then demonstrate how she could drive in them by opening her legs and twisting her feet on the pedals whilst fondling the gear shift, showing off her tanned, Persian-princess-style stocking-tops. For a single guy in Madrid, life could be hard in more ways than one.

Then I met Clem.

29

Grandson of the Marques of somewhere or other, Clemente Peláez told me that he actually descended from Don Pelayo, the first King of Asturias, crowned in 718, and the first Christian hero of the Spanish *Reconquista*. Don Pelayo had refused to accept Islamic rule of his homeland and became a hero after he defeated the Moors at Covadonga in 722. He then died while fighting a bear. The kings of Asturias, León, Castile and Spain itself could trace their lineage back to him for hundreds of years – whilst the eldest son of the King of Spain today is still called the Prince of Asturias. Clemente told me that he also descended from a certain Martin Peláez, who himself was related to the legendary 'El Cid' – the real 'El Cid' that is, not some Charlton Heston-job trying to get his leg over with Sophia Loren.

Clem was an English public-school-educated hooray-Spaniard with slightly floppy blond hair, a long thin face, and just that chinless hint of an upper-class twit about him, but he got away with it through his good sense of humour. He smoked and drank like a fish. And yes, I almost forgot, Clem was also briefly rumoured to have dated 'SAR' (*Su Alteza Real,* which means 'HRH'), La Infanta Doña Elena, one of the king's daughters.

Clem knew everyone in Spain and he was a bit of a maverick himself as, in addition to speaking perfect public-school English, he also spoke perfect *pijo* Spanish.

Pijos, 'pee-ho's' were (and still are) essential to the workings of Spanish society, and once I'd had them identified to me, it was impossible to avoid them. A *pijo,* or *pija,* was a bit like a Spanish 'Sloane', desperately imitating a British aristocrat, with extra weird twists as a result of the Spanish upper classes' close association with Franco's regime.

In my humble opinion, Franco still had an influence over the Spanish consciousness, and whilst modern Spain was certainly no longer just a land of conservative religious beliefs, rigid moral conventions, vast social divisions and violent political conflicts, the memory of Franco's fascist party was still there. Some people described *pijos* as 'rich posh kids' who wore Lacoste or Benetton, but it was much deeper than that, and *pijos* were certainly not all young. True, if you listened carefully, you could hear some teenagers in Madrid saying stuff like, 'This country must have been great under Franco,' but they were just imitating their parents – that older, richer, landed set who were still there after everything Spain had been through. *They* hardly had a bad word to say about the past. Franco was OK as far as they were concerned. Franco paved the way back to a monarchy and restored their status. Franco was (whisper it) a jolly decent chap.

So my interpretation of the whole *pijo* phenomenon was that *pijos* were actually Spaniards who were *frustrated*. Frustrated that someone like Franco was not still around, yet also frustrated and embarrassed that he once *was*. Frustrated that no-one really recognised them – in the sense that they felt they *should* be recognised as being above everyone else. Frustrated that they weren't as aristocratic, royal, rich or landed as they liked to pretend they were. But worst of all, frustrated that they weren't born British aristocrats. You see, accuse a *pijo* of being a *pijo* and they'd deny it. They could be wonderful, charming people, these *pijos* – but their real problem was that they didn't want to be *pijos*. No, they wanted to be the Duke of Norfolk.

And *pijos* felt that they'd only really arrived if they had all the gear on. Their lives evolved around trying to *look* British or royal, or talking about horses, shooting, hunting, or Sotogrande, the tailor-made playground for the *pijo Madrileño* set who moved their homes and Filipino staff down there each summer and then name-dropped all autumn about their latest *íntimos amigos*. It was essential to not only know the right people, but to talk openly about them. And if you couldn't keep up with those conversations, then forget it. If you scratched beneath the surface of the *pijos*, there wasn't much else there at all, and the higher you went up in Spanish society, the higher the *pijo*, and the more frustrated they became.

A number of my new Spanish friends were *pijos*, but I didn't loathe them. I found them hysterical. I found it funny that they never got their confused aristocratic look quite right. A studied carelessness could take generations to perfect, so I often wondered whether *pijos* knew how silly they looked in brand new tweeds, for example, in that heavy bullet-proof quality with shiny leather elbows and trimming on the cuffs. I'd see them shopping in brand new Barbours, with the Barbour badge still pinned on the collar and still wearing them like capes. They wore little bottle-green smock-cardigan felt jackets and navy-blue anoraks with corduroy collars, as if they'd just come in from the estate. Even Hackett had just opened a shop in the heart of the *pijo* area of Salamanca. All this over a decade after the Sloane Ranger had first been identified in London.

The dress code of the female *pijas* was pretty predictable, too. They looked as if they'd just dismounted. They wore imitation jodhpurs, tweed jackets with velvet collars, flat pumps and roll-neck cashmere jumpers – and anything else that looked as if it was from Gucci or Hermès. An equestrian motif also went down well – like a silk scarf with stirrups all over it, which they could then knot around the handle of their imitation 'Kelly' handbags. And to crown it all, years after Princess Diana had worn one, the 'Big Velvet Hairband' had finally hit Spain – in 1992! If you popped into the Loewe shop in Serrano, you'd see giant horsey assistants in giant velvet hairbands, greeting you with giant haughty voices and eyeing you up and down to see if you belonged. They spoke not with plums in their mouths, but with lisps. They scared the crap out of me, to be honest. They always slipped an 'f' in after the 's', as in *'buenasf diasf'*. It was very hard to shop there with a straight face.

In fact, the entire *pijo* shopping experience was bizarre. In the decoration shops of Salamanca, I'd see Spaniards snap up English-embossed 'wine cellar record' and 'visitors' books or foxhunting coasters and tablemats while *Brideshead* music was piped gently in the background. And now that Marks & Spencer had also finally arrived, I'd see armies of *pijos* in the food department each Saturday, stocking up on such delights as tartan boxes of shortbread and Olde English marmalade, all pretending *not to be* Spanish in their sleeveless Puffa jackets and bullet-proof tweeds.

The tweeds may have been new, but they signified o-l-d: old Spain, old friends, old houses, old furniture, old wine, old family, old money, old blood. And old blood and pedigree didn't exclude bullfighters. Bullfighting was to *pijos* what foxhunting was to most Sloanes: it simply *had* to be defended even if they didn't necessarily admit to participating in it personally. Bullfighters may have seemed cruel and naff to the average package tourist, but they were often from 'good families', *'buenas familias'*. Bulls and bullfighting meant farms, *fincas*, horses, estates, land, olives, sherry, money. The obsession with *buenas familias* was an echo of the old Spanish obsession with the 'thoroughbred' pure race, *'pura raza'*, and pure blood, *'pura sangre'*, an obsession that was about as *pijo* as you could get. The family of the Duke of Alba, for example, famous in the sixteenth century for terrorising Dutch protestants, still exists today. And the eighteenth Duchess of Alba, the young daughter in that most titled of aristocratic European families, is married to … a *bullfighter*.

Clem was not your average run-of-the-mill *pijo*, though. Clem and his mates were above and beyond *pijo*. They were 'ultra-*pijos*'.

Clem and his work colleagues first came into my life in late 1990. Clem worked for a company called Publicom, based in a tiny, grotty office somewhere off the Castellana, near the Bernabéu. Publicom specialised in the 'marketing and commercialisation' of sport – and in particular polo. Why polo? Because polo was the hobby of Clem and his partners, who were the brothers (of four polo-playing brothers), Iñaki and Vicente Prado, together with Felipe de Villapadierna. To me, they were just four pissheads who never had any money in their pockets and who became great friends. But they were all from ultra-*pijo* families. The Prado brothers' uncle was the renowned Manuel Prado y Colón de Carvajal, a close friend of King Juan Carlos. Felipe's father, meanwhile, was the 'legendary Count', the Conde de Villapadierna, most famous, according to Clem, for his supposed romance with Rita bloody Hayworth. But then what Spaniard *hadn't* rogered Rita, or even more so 'our Ava', as they called Ava Gardner?

As for Clem himself, I finally realised there was something different about him the day we went to a Cartier party together. We'd both received invitations – mine, through *Vogue*, and his, apparently, through his own social network. As always, though, he never actually showed me his invitation, so I never really knew if he had one. It was always, 'Oh, I've been invited there, too,' whenever I mentioned a party – which was fine, because he was great company.

When we arrived at the Cartier bash at the refurbished Madrid Casino, we hovered on the red carpet inside, eyeing the totty following us in, helping ourselves to several glasses of champagne, when the strangest thing happened. Reacting to a huge commotion at the door, the society photographers started flashing away at the grand entrance of someone *muy importante*. It turned out to be one of the king's two sisters – Doña Pilar, it was, the big round one, although I think both sisters were quite big and round – but this was the one who wasn't big, round *and* blind. When she saw Clem, she suddenly stopped her little entourage and reached out to kiss him on both cheeks with, *'Hola, Clemente* – lovely to see you again …'

Clem just beamed at her. I pretended not to notice, though. I didn't want to give him such pleasure because he kept doing this. A night out with Clem was like a night out with Alfie Stokes – if you know the joke. Alfie Stokes knew everyone, right up to appearing on the balcony with the Pope at the Vatican, where two New Zealand tourists gazed up from St.Peter's Square, saying, 'Who's that git up there in the purple robe next to Alfie?'

I'd met Iñaki Prado first, and then Clem, Vicente and Felipe. Iñaki had come to see me to propose that *Vogue* sponsor a polo tournament in Madrid, trying to convince me of all the benefits for our brand to be associated with the sport of kings. But our new commercial director, José Luis, being a Spaniard himself, could see that Iñaki was a rich kid, and didn't want to do business with him. It was definitely going to need an outsider, an *Englishman*, to get it all off the ground – with a little help from the Persian princess. So I decided to do it with *Casa Vogue* instead of *Vogue*, and then we didn't really sponsor it but made money out of it instead, by selling the names of the six teams involved to clients such as Mercedes, Iberia and Chopard, and then charging them over the odds for a double page 'advertorial' in our polo promotion.

Besides, it looked like we'd finally exhausted all other methods of trying to make *Casa Vogue* work. Things were getting tougher, and the feeling was that once the 1992 summer party was over, we were going to hit a recession as fast as the trots erupt after a salmonella-*paella*.

It is not easy to organise a polo tournament in Spain, especially if you speak piss-poor Spanish, and especially if you're dealing with a bunch of *locos* all the time. The invitations, the shirts, the marquees, the cocktail party, the guest list – even the cup itself, which Giovanni and I bought and got engraved at a little trophy shop tucked away in Jorge Juan. The whole event took place over three evenings during the last week of June. The midweek games gave us a chance to practise our cocktail-*ito* facilities so that by the Saturday evening, they were perfect. It was a massive relief when it was all over – and in a sense, I started to feel as if I could achieve anything in Spain.

That feeling was endorsed, firstly by Luis when he promoted me to *Director Gerente*, and then, sixteen hours after the polo final, mid-afternoon on Sunday, when I finally christened the sun-beds to join the Spanish Federation of Sexology Societies' *siesta*-shagging statistics, by playing a glorious game of open-air 'hide the *chorizo*' under a blazing sun on my *terraza*, with a *ninfómana* called Nicola, a travelling Australian I'd met during polo week.

In fact, finally and unexpectedly, I was able to embark on what Adolfo called a 'minjay binjay', that lasted all summer and well into the autumn, thanks to the horny Patrizia, who steered me wonderfully back on course. I met her on one of those suffocating Madrid summer evenings, midweek, mid-July. The terrace bars in the Costa Castellana were heaving with scantily-clad *Madrileñas* as Spain moved into that wonderful last fortnight of July when minds, bodies and attitudes were already gearing up for the August shutdown, when factories and offices operated with skeleton staff during the *hora intensiva*, all winding down for the forthcoming *operación salida*. I'd played tennis with Daniel and then we'd hit the Castellana 8 bar, where we bumped into a girlfriend of his together with the tanned, mini-skirted, petite Patrizia. She wasn't exactly the type of girl you'd take home to meet your mum – I mean, Patrizia was filthy-looking – but from the moment I met her and quickly deduced that she wasn't disappearing on the *operación salida* herself, it was perfect timing. And this time she was a *Madrileña*.

You see, I had a permanently warm, tickling sensation in my guts at that moment. It wasn't just the job – or the sun, my *terraza*, the spare cash, or the *señoritas*.

It was *Madrid*.

It was Madrid that was making me walk around with a permanent smile on my face and practically a permanent hard-on. Madrid had totally seduced me. I started to wonder why I'd ever worried about missing out on an olive farm or lounging on a Mediterranean beach. There was just something incredibly sexy about being *anywhere* in Spain at that time, with the Olympic torch about to ignite the fuse to the whole nation's collective libido.

30

The Catalans know how to throw a party and 'The Barcelona '92 Games of the XXV Olympiad' was the biggest they'd ever attempted. 'Barcelona is the city of the whole world!' shouted Mayor Maragall at the opening ceremony to rapturous, wild applause.

The ceremony itself didn't start until eight in the evening, but by then, I was well-oiled and considerably *caliente* – to use the word I'd once used on María Teresa to describe how 'hot' I was feeling. I was in fucking flames again. There were 70,000 in the stadium with an estimated 4,000 million watching on TV, and it all opened with a huge flock of doves and walking puppets representing the Rambla of Barcelona. I was ecstatic, half-watching it on TV from my candlelit *terraza*, uncorking more bubbly to the sound of Alfredo Kraus singing, *'Del cabello más sutil'*. By the time the king was invited to open the Games, I had the petite, kinky Patrizia firmly in my arms. The Olympic torch arrived and was used to set light to … an arrow! The lights went out and a Paralympic archer finally took his stand, before firing the flaming arrow across the sky to ignite the Olympic cauldron. Out on the candlelit *terraza*, I was about to attempt something similar myself.

Do you know what the highlight of the Games was, the biggest surprise of all? No, not Linford Christie's bollocks slapping uncontrollably from thigh to thigh during his hundred-metre gold. No, the *real* highlight of the Games and the most embarrassing, was that the Spanish themselves won far too many medals, almost as if it was fixed. Right from the opening day with the twenty-kilometre silly walk, it was a Spaniard, Señor Plaza, who won gold, putting an already frenzied nation into a state of even higher euphoria that didn't stop until the closing ceremony. Spain won thirteen golds (compared to five over the previous ninety-two years), seven silver and two bronze medals in total, including a gold for beating the poor Poles in football, which I thought was pretty inhospitable.

My summer with Patrizia ended after a carnal finale in one of the most beautiful hotels in Spain, in Carmona, a small town near Seville. Back in Madrid, she broached the idea of me meeting her parents, so that she could then move all her things onto my roof with me. I realised our time was up.

In September 1992, Luis then sent me first-class to New York for a get-together of colleagues from other European operations at Condé Nast's Madison Avenue HQ. We went berserk for ninety-six hours, chauffeured around in a black limo uptown and downtown – out on the Circle Line ferry to the Statue of Liberty, up the Empire State, out to a Broadway show, out to the Russian Tea Room, the Palm restaurant, and even an Italian joint where Woody Allen surreally sat, as though in one of his own films, on the table beside us. Most of these get-togethers were organised by a nice enough chap called Peter Armour, who had a bit of a nervous twitch, and which seemed to get steadily worse as he frowned heavily on all our drinking and smoking. His title was something like the 'Senior Executive Chief Corporate Vice-President (*open brackets*) Creative Circulation Strategic Consumer Marketing Research Operating Officer (*close brackets*)' – and thus he took himself *very* seriously indeed.

In fact the whole Condé Nast New York culture was so different to Madrid. I couldn't see how I was going to apply any of their 'Database Marketing Strategies' to my distribution chief, José Luis. We didn't even have a computer installed at Sir Rhino Twes. As for having 'dress-down Fridays' or 'stand-up only meetings' or 'non-alcoholic lunches' – well, that would have all gone down like lead balloons tied to the testicles of a soon-to-be tossed goat back in Spain, wouldn't it? I couldn't – I mean, I didn't even *dare* – tell 'Vice-President Pete' that a client lunch in Madrid could last over four hours and that if he expected your average *Madrileño* oaf – one of those spinning-top-shaped ravenous fatsos – to sit through it all *and* have-a-nice-day without a bottle of Rioja or two followed by a cigar and a *coñac*, then he must have been out of his New-York-state-of-mind.

The American theme then continued back in Madrid when Clem introduced me to Margaux Hemingway.

'Tim, Margaux,' he said, with a big grin. 'Margaux, Tim.'

'Hello, Margaux,' I said.

Well, you would, wouldn't you? I mean, it's not often you're in Madrid and you get introduced to one of Ernest Hemingway's granddaughters, is it? It all seemed so appropriate. Clem couldn't have done any better, apart from exhuming Ava Gardner. And you know what was going through my mind? Was *she* the one? Would this be it? Was I destined to marry Margaux Hemingway? The answer was no.

Of course I wasn't.

She wasn't bad, though, was Margaux. I mean, her teeth and eyes were all lovely but she seemed to have a hairy sort of fluffy face when you got up close. Don't ask me how Clem had rustled up Margaux for a weekend in Madrid, but somehow he had. I think it was something to do with a polo tournament in which his old friend La Infanta Doña Elena attended, and which an American airline sponsored on the condition that an American celebrity was present. Crafty Clem had therefore struck a deal with a rent-a-celebrity agency in Florida. He'd hoped to get polo-*aficionados* such as Stephanie Powers or Sylvester Stallone to jet over, but had to make do with Margaux Hemingway instead.

So Margaux had to make do with me.

I went for drinks with Clem, Margaux and a girl-friend of hers who'd also flown over, at the newly-opened Santo Mauro hotel in Zurbano where they were staying. Immediately, though, Margaux started talking gibberish about therapy and potions and stuff, which bored the arse off me until she also said she 'self-hypnotised' in the mirror.

'I stare at myself until my face changes and I see messages …'

'*I've* done that!' I cried, taking a swig of beer while being watched warily by Clem. It's true, I had, countless times in foul-smelling gents' loos, immediately after vomiting.

'Have you?' she said, pushing her fluffy face closer to mine. '*Have* you? Isn't it just an amazing, exhilarating, sexy experience?'

'It is,' I squeaked. Her face was extremely close to mine.

'How often do you do it?' she purred. 'Do you also see messages?'

'Well,' I explained. 'It's not that I do it that often, you know, but –'

Clem had had enough. He interrupted, and the

evening came to an abrupt end before Margaux could say, 'Let's do it together, naked, upstairs in my suite, whilst sipping Dom Pérignon, and then let's fly first class to LA, where you can then inherit all Papa Ernest's estate.'

Instead, two hours later, alone at home and scratching my *cojones*, I zapped the TV channels to find a bullfight at Madrid's Las Ventas, just as the camera panned round the so-called celebrities in the crowd, suddenly picking out Margaux and … *Clem*, sitting side-by-side. The commentator said, 'How interesting it is to see Hemingway's granddaughter in the crowd.' But I zapped away before I could see Clem, no doubt with a smug look on his face, waving at me from the TV.

31

Soon after meeting Margaux, Clem and I bonded further with the help of two New York models whom we came across in Pachá, having overheard them talking at the bar.

'*Vuh-vogue!*' Clem had slurred. 'You're *Vogue* models, shuh-surely?' '*We're* from *Vuhogue!*' he continued, lecherously.

We? He'd obviously been practising this, but it worked, and he managed to swing the girls away from the Pachá bar to a table the other side of the dancefloor. They *were* models but not *Vogue* models, although they *wanted to be*: they just hadn't had any luck in getting anyone at Sir Rhino Twes to see them. They'd been told that it would be easy to get modelling jobs in Spain to pad out their portfolios, and I'd understood this was the norm, which is why Condé Nast Spain benefited from cheaper fees and some of our models looked crap. So I arranged an appointment for them at our offices, although they never heard from *Vogue* again. It didn't matter, because they were forever grateful, and this meant Clem and I could take them out to La Parra, a beautiful Seville-style restaurant in Monte Esquinza. The problem we had was that Clem had organised two evenings in one – not unusual for Madrid, and certainly not unusual for Clem, who ran a dozen social circles at once. Tonight, while we were absolutely convinced that we were going to get laid, Clem had complicated arrangements by insisting we first call in at a cocktail party held by one of the main terrestrial TV channels.

At the party I knew someone Clem knew, an Italian called Yolanda Manfredi. There was a large contingent of Italians in Madrid and whenever there was something Italian going on, Yolanda was in the middle of it. So Yolanda knew a lot of people, among whom was Antonia dell'Atte, an Italian model with sharp, spiky, sparkling features. I think she modelled for Armani but other than that, she was a nobody, or still would be if her bounder of an Italian husband, Alessandro Lequio, hadn't ran off with a trashy TV-actress called Ana Obregón. This affair was quickly labelled the '*Culebrón* Obregón', as *culebrón* meant soap-opera, and Ana Obregón was a walking one.

The story was this: Ana Obregón decided to rob Antonia dell'Atte of her husband. But instead of going back to Italy with her tail between her legs, Antonia fought back – not for her husband, but for her own pride. She had a vicious, funny, scathing Italian tongue, and said exactly what she thought and for that reason, the Spanish media adored her. Shortly before the Antenna 3 party, she had appeared on a TV programme called *La Máquina de la Verdad*, (*The Truth Machine*), one of the very first reality shows in which a celebrity was wired up to a lie-detector machine. The Spanish loved it and overnight, Antonia became the most famous person in Spain. So when Clem and I turned up outside Yolanda's house to give her a lift to the party that night, we were wildly over-excited when she said we *also* had to 'pick up Antonia'.

'*Ciaaaoooo*, *Yannndaaa!*' screeched Antonia, having squeezed into the front of my Golf. Clem had moved into the back with Yolanda, who'd now become *Yannndaaa*. Antonia had kissed us on every cheek she could find, then draped herself across my lap with her palm on my crotch as she checked herself in the mirror. She didn't talk, she yapped.

Fifteen minutes later, and we were mingling with guests waiting to enter the grand party at the *Palacio de los Congresos*. Clem and I tried to separate ourselves from Yolanda and Antonia, but by the time it was our turn to walk up the red carpet, Yolanda had latched onto Clem, leaving me helplessly with the hyper Italian. In one huge sweeping gesture, she waltzed me up the steps arm-in-arm as I frantically ducked my head, trying to tuck my whole chubby face under my collar against the barrage of flashbulbs. Just as quickly as the cameras focused on her entering the party, they left her alone when she was inside. And once Antonia could see that the spotlight had been turned off, as quickly, too, did she discard me for the richer, slimmer, chiselled TV-execs, and I was thrown to one side with a final, *'Ciao, Teeem ...'*

Carried away by this tawdry taste of celebrity air-kissing, Clem and I must have over-lubricated ourselves somewhere along the way before the dinner later that same night with our two New York models. It was a total disaster. We *arrived* pissed, and in that classic Madrid way, dinner was followed by drinks at a bar, then drinks at another bar, then drinks at a club – and by two in the morning we were trying to work the models slowly back towards my Serrano roof in a straight line, but ended up at a music-bar nearby. Now the models stood out as tall, attractive *guiris*, and Clem and I stood out like a couple of *gilipollas* (dickheads, remember), and the bar had an evil, aggressive feel to it – maybe because it was close to the Bernabéu stadium and it was a fanatical supporters' bar or something. Either way, the four of us looked out of place, and soon enough matters kicked off. I was at the bar when I saw four guys antagonising poor Clem, pointing and poking him in the face, even spitting. All I could see was one of the guys with a bottle of beer curling in his hand behind his back and there I was, thirty-two years old, flying across the room with the sole intention of connecting my fist with the guy clasping that bottle – and then when it *did* half-connect, he looked as surprised as me. Immediately, it was chaos. As I was pushed to the floor and kicked, I heard smashing glass and saw Clem pounced on by several others. Then suddenly it was like one of those Wild West movies, where a mass fight breaks out just because two guys have had an argument. I remember thinking, *why – why –* as I crashed to the floor, *why* were those people over *there* also taking part? But that wasn't really the worst of it. The *real* problem was that we lost the girls in the Mexican saloon-style mêlée because they jumped into a taxi back to their *hostal*, never to be seen again.

And Madrid is a village.

'I didn't see you on TV with Antonia dell'Atte, did I?' Sylvia asked on the Monday morning, as she brought me a *café con leche.*

'No,' I said, still shaking and sweating from what had become a forty-eight hour binge with Clem. I wasn't sure if I could drink a coffee without spilling it. I wondered just how far down the slippery slope I had slid. I was pushing my luck. I'd tried to stop bingeing and partying after my *infarto* scare but, having met Clem, I now seemed to be worse than ever. I was contemplating the prospects of dismissal and being sent packing back to Brixton with rising dread, when the blonde from the *Vogue* fashion room suddenly appeared at my doorway.

I'd bumped into her before, when I'd gone with Clem to yet another Italian party organised by Yolanda. It had been at the Palacio de Gaviria for the

Grupo Piaggio-Vespa, hosted by Giovanni Agnelli, who had just moved to Madrid to run the scooter company. Giovanni was the twenty-eight year old nephew of the *'avocatto'* himself, Gianni Agnelli (who I think *also* rogered Rita Hayworth), and was thus the heir apparent of the family dynasty, the 'crown prince of Fiat'. He'd greeted Clem profusely, of course, because somehow they both knew one another, but I didn't ask how, I couldn't face it.

'Did you and Clemente Peláez get in a fight in a club over the weekend?' the blonde now asked, standing in the doorway.

'How do *you* know Clem?' I groaned, but it was a stupid question. She knew Yolanda, who knew Antonia, who knew Clem, who knew everyone.

'Ana Maria van Pallandt' from the *Vogue* fashion department, it transpired, was an ex-'muse' of Valentino. We'd all ogled her along the corridors at the office, and in the lift, and we'd even all walked slowly past the fashion room, quickly turning our heads to catch a glimpse of her stacking shoe-boxes or sorting out the clothes-rails, but none of us had ever dared speak to her, as although she looked like a million dollars, she seemed a bit of an ice-queen, too.

The reason I'd seen her at the Piaggio-Vespa party was that she was actually dating Giovanni Agnelli, which as Clem and even Luis pointed out, placed her 'out of bounds'. But as she spoke English, Ana Maria started to come into my office every morning to chat or borrow the latest magazines. I never got a word in, and never learnt much about her other than the latest gossip from the fashion room. But she slowly became a friend, and eventually, with Clem, we even went to a bullfight at Aranjuez with Agnelli and all had dinner. And then I met her sister.

32

I could feel myself going love-struck pink with embarrassment when I first met Kirsa van Pallandt.

'I Want To Marry Those Legs,' I thought.

Kirsa had actually just joined the company alongside her sister, and Luis had already met her and told me that I should keep my eyes out for her.

'Qué bella,' he'd drooled. *'Bellisima.* Beautiful. I've finally found the girl for you …'

The first time I plucked up courage to telephone Kirsa at her flat, a voice bellowed down the phone in English with an American accent:

'HELLO!'

'Kirsa?'

'NO!'

'Who's that then?' I said.

'NINA!' Then: 'WHO THE FUCK IS *THAT*?'

'Oh,' I said, feeling extremely English all of a sudden. 'I beg your pardon?'

'I said, who the *fuck* is that?'

'It's only me. *Teeem Parfeeee.*'

'ARF-WHAAAT?' she roared, as if she was exploding.

'Parfeeee.'

'FARTEEE?'

'Er ... I'll call back later. Thank you.' Click.

When Kirsa somehow managed to call *me* back, I asked her whether her flatmate had given her the message.

'What flatmate? I don't have a flatmate.'

'So, who's Nina?'

'That's my mom,' she laughed.

'No way.'

'Well, it *is.* Yep – Nina's definitely a mom.'

I knew that she was half-Dutch and half-Danish, but I didn't really *know* Kirsa, even though she'd worked on some of our polo layouts and even accompanied me to a presentation. I hadn't been able to keep my eyes off her endless legs brushing against mine in the back of a sweaty *Madrileño* taxi, but I'd assumed she was also out of bounds. It took six months before we actually went out for a meal together. When a date was finally set, organised by her sister, Ana Maria, I wanted to know who else was going to be there.

'Couples,' came the reply.

So I then asked who they were pairing me off with.

'Me,' joked Kirsa. Or at least I thought it was a joke.

A week later, though – and so typical of the

Madrileño social life – all I ever heard from Ana Maria was that she was still having problems trying to organise the dinner for us all. At first it was scheduled for the Friday, then cancelled, then rearranged again, then cancelled, then finally postponed until the following Friday when we were all to go for a Japanese – but then this was of course cancelled at the last minute again. I was surprised at how disappointed I felt. I was mulling this over and promising myself that one day I'd pluck up the courage to ask Kirsa for dinner myself, when suddenly she marched her long legs into my office.

'My sister can't get her act together to organise anything,' she huffed. 'I was looking forward to a Japanese. Shall we go together?'

I was speechless. Then something very odd shot out of my mouth before I could stop it. 'No,' it said. 'I don't like Japanese food.'

'Oh,' said Kirsa. 'It's strange that you never mentioned that before.'

'It is,' said the voice again. 'It's bloody strange.'

Then there was an awful silence before something even worse emanated from the depths of my throat. I could feel it coming, I could even hear it loud and clear when it finally arrived, but I couldn't believe it was my own voice. 'I can't go out tonight anyway,' it said.

'Oh …' started Kirsa.

'But I *can* tomorrow,' I added, before the other voice could ruin my life forever.

'Tomorrow?'

'Yes. Ever been to the Teatriz?'

We went out for dinner to my favourite restaurant with its Philippe Starck-raving-mad décor. She looked beautiful, even more so when she laughed and her whole face creased up. She smoked and drank enough, thank God. She touched my arm several times to make a point. I loved that. She sat sideways in her chair to face me. I loved that, too. I learnt that her parents, now divorced, had been singers, and from the late fifties right through to the late sixties, they'd entertained audiences across the globe with their sweet harmonies and pop-slanted folk and calypso songs as 'Nina and Frederik'. Kirsa herself had been born in Málaga because her parents were renovating an old *finca* in Ibiza, and then, as they were always on tour and doing TV shows, she lived with nannies in Switzerland, then London, then Los Angeles, then Cape Town, then Los Angeles again, then Ibiza, then finally Madrid. After her parents split up and Nina started her solo career, Kirsa had gone to high school in Hollywood. Her mother, she added, had been in a few Robert Altman movies and *American Gigolo* in which she called Richard Gere a cocksucking-motherfucker in her opening line. So I'd escaped lightly in my telephone encounter with her.

In between all this, she showed me some Polaroids from a shoot she'd been doing that day. I reminded myself that this was why we were there – friends from work having dinner, nothing else. But I was hooked. So much so that when she let slip that she had two young kids, Clara and Adrian, and an ex-husband who was some kind of has-been Spanish soap-actor, it didn't make the slightest bit of difference. When I dropped her off after dinner, then got home myself, I sat up and drank more wine until the early hours, in a state, if one exists, of total, *utter* besottedment. I could still smell her perfume.

33

'I thought you might want to see this before Luis does,' said the matronly María Teresa, after creeping into my office early one morning and gently shutting the door behind her. She was holding open a magazine and looked concerned about something as she placed it on my desk, right under my nose. I waited for the inevitable tongue-twister, but there was nothing. Something was definitely wrong.

'What's up?' I said, instinctively flicking the magazine closed to see the cover.

It wasn't unusual for María Teresa to bring magazines in for me. In fact I think she received every publication ever printed in Spain, thumbing through them meticulously for anything about Condé Nast or *Vogue* worldwide that she could cut out for her archives. She often brought in foreign magazines, too – not just from our own group, but anything that Luis thought I should take a look at. But there was something different about her demeanour that morning, and certainly something different about the magazine she'd plonked in front of me. It was the weekly *Diez Minutos*, which meant 'Ten Minutes', and it was one of those *¡Hola!*-style magazines, crueller, cheaper, poorer-quality, more mass-market, and which took less than ten minutes to read.

Owned by Condé Nast's rivals, Hachette, *Diez Minutos* was one of Spain's established celebrity-gossip magazines in the sector known as 'the heart press', *la prensa de corazón* – an essential lifeline for the Spanish *paparazzi*, and which included *Lecturas, Semana, ¡Hola!, Pronto* and *Interviú*. The 'heart press' was a phenomenon in Spain. Some said its origins could be traced back to the harsh repression that followed the civil war which left few families unscathed, and thus considerable vigilance was required as people avoided giving anything away that might betray them. So a love of harmless gossip, *cotilleo*, was born, whereby Spaniards gossiped about the rich and famous as they sought escapism from daily life. In a nation that read, per capita, less than one book per year, 'the heart press' comprised the staple diet of Spain's reading matter among a high proportion of the population. As the newspapers weren't tabloids, the *cotilleo* magazines had a ball – and every TV channel also had at least one programme devoted to the world of *los famosas* – although 'famous' for what, I was never sure.

María Teresa flicked open *Diez Minutos* in front of me again, and, as I gazed towards the pages she was pointing at, I felt as if I recognised something but I couldn't quite put my finger on it. But then – *oh, shit!* – it suddenly hit me. I was looking at Kirsa and – and – me! Oh, no! How fucking awful! How *bloody embarrassing!* María Teresa could sense my horror, and she immediately put her big meaty arm around me to console me.

Why the hell would anyone want to see photos of us – Kirsa and *me*, a fatty, flatulent Brit? The photos showed us walking down a street, probably on the way back from a clandestine midweek lunch. I scanned the captions to the photos in front of María Teresa (who was now laughing a little) and I noticed that they hadn't even spelt our names right. Kirsa was 'Kirtand' and I was 'Thimotty Porfitt'! Who the hell was Thimotty fucking Porfitt? Poor fit? It seemed almost appropriate.

It just shows how desperate the 'heart press' could be. Just because Kirsa was beautiful, and her parents were once singers, and she was the 'ex' of some actor, *Diez Minutos* decided to announce that she was 'going out with a work colleague' who was an 'English *ejecutivo*' and 'who'd also become her sentimental companion'. How cringe-making is that? Under another heading of, 'Kirtand has a new *lurrvve*', it went on to say that Kirtand's kids, who were Clara (seven) and Adrian (four), had 'taken very affectionately to Thimotty'.

Even without me around, the *paparazzi* still stalked Kirsa in and out of work, out on the school run and down to the El Corte Inglés supermarket car-park to

A Load of Bull

... photograph her loading her shopping in the car! She finally lost her cool one day, screaming at them to leave her the fuck alone whilst waving a family-pack of loo-paper, and yelling whether they wanted to know the make of it. They didn't, though. They just wanted to take pictures. And this went on for ages, and we just had to ignore it until eventually it went away ... almost.

Our relationship had been uncovered the day Kirsa had brought the kids into the office late one afternoon and, having had to rush off with Adrian, she'd asked me to take little Clara home.

'*Timmy!*' shouted Clara, just ten minutes later, skipping off happily down the corridor in search of me, having been colouring in the art department. '*Timmy!*' she yelled, as the two advertising secretaries, Mayte and Vicky, poked their nosy heads out of their office.

'*Timmy?*' they asked. 'Why are you looking for Timmy?'

'Because he's taking me home,' she explained, innocently enough.

'Why's Timmy taking you home?' asked Mayte, rather concerned.

'Because he sleeps with my mummy, stupid!' yelled Clara, aged seven, skipping on ahead.

34

Kirsa was twenty-nine. I was thirty-two and had 'inherited' her two kids. The reality of this hit me early on, when I felt what I believed to be Kirsa's warm, sensuous hand in the middle of the night, gently edging its way across my naked belly where it started to softly stroke and tickle my navel, before cleverly making its way down towards my private zone, nestling hesitantly on my pubes before suddenly thumping me very hard in the *cojones.*

'Jeezus! What the hell was that for?' I groaned, grabbing her hand and tugging it away from my bollocks only to discover that it wasn't Kirsa's hand at all. It was Adrian's left foot ... bless him.

Whilst these little obstacles quickly became part of my new life, and whilst I accepted them as a bonus of having fallen in love with Kirsa, it took time for others to believe it. 'You're *what?*' was the response I first received when I announced to friends that I was going to marry a divorcee with two kids. But I was very lucky.

I was very lucky that the kids' real father didn't seem to want to know. This allowed me to fill a gap and they embraced me from day one. In fact, it wasn't so much that I inherited them, but *they* adopted *me*.

I moved in with Kirsa, Clara and Adrian in January 1993, to another rented *ático* flat, a little bit like mine but with living space rather than just roof space. It was still in Salamanca, in Calle de Povedilla, at number 13, parallel to Calle de Goya. Povedilla 13 should be pronounced 'po-buh-diya trethé', but even after all these years, it came out of my *guiri* mouth as 'Popper-deeya-tweshey'. This is what I said the first time Clara excitedly accompanied me in a taxi.

'Popper qué?' came the reply.

Clara corrected my pronunciation and in her perfect Spanish, announced to the driver, 'Don't take any notice of him. He's English. He doesn't speak Spanish very well. *Esta hacienda el chorra,*' – which meant, 'He's just playing silly buggers.'

Soon after I moved to Povedilla 13, I finally got to meet Nina, too, who greeted me with, 'Hi, I'm the old bat!' We took her to the Teatriz, where I asked her if I could marry her daughter. She yelled, 'Of course you fucking can!' Then she started to cry.

So Kirsa cried.

I even cried.

Nina had her own flat in Madrid and occasionally babysat, which allowed us to sometimes disappear for whole weekends ... which meant that early on, we drove down to stay at the Casa de Carmona near Seville, one of Spain's top romantic hideaways. Kirsa loved it – the décor, the candles, the log-fires, the ice-cold bubbly, the little exquisite touches, the complete and utter *romance* of that old sixteenth century palace with its beautifully decorated rooms and furnishings. We stayed two nights, taking a day trip out through the olive fields and *pueblos blancos* to lunch high up in Ronda, strolling over the Puente Nuevo to the Museo Taurino at the Plaza de Toros before heading back to our log-fire nest in Carmona. There was only one snag in all of this. I'd been there before with the filthy Patrizia. I'd nearly got away with it, though – until we checked out. The receptionist started tapping away at her computer whilst looking at my credit card, and suddenly came out with, 'I hope you enjoyed your stay with us *again, Señor Parfeee.*'

There was an embarrassed, uncomfortable silence.

'You never said you'd been here before,' said Kirsa, rather sharply.

'I'll just put the bags in the car ...' I said, hurrying out.

My bachelor days and my *Madrileño* yuppie phase were over. At last I'd found more than just that elusive leggy blonde. I'd found a beautiful woman who didn't need me to pretend to be a 'you-pee' with *gomina*-caked hair anymore. We wouldn't need the Philippe Starck lemon-squeezer either. She'd be happy squeezing all the fruit herself and making marmalade for the rest of her life, if necessary, just as long as she could do so as near to the Mediterranean as possible. My Golf was soon swapped for a kids'-sick-stained Volvo.

At the office, we tried to keep out of one another's way but it wasn't easy. Whenever there was a work-related social event (which was often), Luis always insisted I brought her along. So Kirsa started to accompany me to many *Vogue fiestas* and Condé Nast 'tasks', from cocktails at embassies to dinners at Casa Lucio. In fact, despite María Teresa's fear of what Luis would say when the relationship between 'Kirtand' and that tubby 'Thimotty Porfitt' first surfaced in the weekly *Diez Minutos*, he was fairly relaxed about it. And in his own sly way, I think he was even quite *proud*. When he'd first heard, he'd pushed his sliding-doors shut, patted me on the shoulders with both hands, then asked me to take a seat before saying in that *Godfather* drawl, 'She's *muy guapa*. You're very lucky.'

35

By the summer of 1993 the recession had finally hit Spain. The Madrid stock market had declined thirty per cent in the previous year, and foreign investment had plummeted. Felipe González had just been returned as Prime Minister in the June 1993 general election with a severely diminished majority amid serious criticism about economic mismanagement, growing unemployment, corruption, cronyism and incompetence in high circles, just a year after the 1992 bonanza. Everywhere you looked, there was a scandal being unearthed, from the disgraced 'beautiful people' and businessmen such as Mario Conde and Javier de la Rosa to the former governor of the Bank of Spain, Mariano Rubio, who got jailed for financial malfeasance, to the former head of the Guardia Civil, a slippery little bugger called Luis Roldán, who'd disappeared with over ten million quid of secret funds normally used to pay informants and the widows of slain policemen. There was a young judge called Baltasar Garzón who was constantly in the news trying to expose most of these scams, but the more he unearthed, the more links appeared to members of the PSOE itself – and because few offenders from the powerful élite ever got convicted, most Spaniards became increasingly cynical. It was chaos. Whilst González himself was in the clear, Spain – Europe's fastest growing economy for much, if not all of the eighties – now seemed to have been run by nothing more than a bunch of crooks. There were moments when I wondered whether my own time in the country was also up.

The decision to close *Casa Vogue* was no surprise to me because I'd suggested it to Luis in the first place. We'd tried sexier covers, special giveaways, everything, but nothing had worked. When the decision was made to close it, and knowing we would have to let several people go, including the editor, I suggested that I should perhaps leave as well, but Luis just laughed. He hit me with the task of running the office in Barcelona instead, as well as planning the editorial for our first Spanish *GQ*.

I quickly discovered that no-one in Spain could pronounce *GQ*.

'*Hey Koo.*'

'No, no, look at the letters. Look: *GQ*.'

'*Hey Koo.*'

'No, no. Look. *GQ*. Got it? *Geee ... queue. Geee ... queue*. Got it? You try it.'

'Hey Koo.'

If you knew your Spanish alphabet, then you'd know that *GQ* would come out as, *'Hey Koo'*, which was nonsensical, and even more so if you explained that *GQ* really stood for *Gentlemen's Quarterly*. Everything was fine when our men's magazine was a mere supplement to Spanish *Vogue*, when we happily called it *Vogue Hombre* – or *Vogue Man*. But once we changed the name in preparation for its launch as a stand-alone title, it soon became apparent that no-one could pronounce the bloody thing. I hadn't expected this. But a brand is a brand, however it's pronounced around the globe. I suggested that we should devise a fun campaign based around *GQ* being the magazine that Spaniards couldn't pronounce – you know: 'The magazine that's impossible to ask for at the news-kiosks, so subscribe to it now and save yourself the embarrassment.' The rest of the staff looked at me as if I was a raving fucking lunatic.

Our Barcelona sales office occupied a grand amount of ornately-tiled floor space in the Rambla de Cataluña – one of the first things Luis ordered me to downscale. It was full of avant-garde Catalan office furniture, too, beautifully designed but totally impractical. There was something wonderfully bizarre about Catalan designers, especially their furniture. The chairs looked fantastic in the shops along Paseo de Gràcia, but, my God, were they uncomfortable.

I'd inherited five employees: Yolanda, Lourdes,

Renato, Marta and Susanna. Yolanda was bossy, with thick auburn curly hair. She bit her bottom lip to stop herself laughing at my accent. Lourdes was the happy, smiling and efficient general assistant. Renato was a shy, studious Brazilian. Marta was great, our Giovanni*esque* matriarch figure for Barcelona, a sparkling personality who was half-Andaluz, half-Catalan. Susanna was, well, sultry.

Our office soon went from strength to strength, so much so that Jonathan alternated his monthly visits between Madrid and Barcelona, flying in for the night for a following day's meeting, while Luis flew over to join us on the *puente aéreo*. We normally took Jonathan to the Set Portes restaurant in the Passeig d'Isabel II, where he'd rip apart the bread rolls before tucking hungrily into his new favourite dish of *arroz negro*, that thick black rice cooked in squid's ink. I had to walk him around the outside of Gaudí's floodlit 'unfinished cathedral', the Sagrada Família, at midnight, as Luis waited drowsily in a taxi nearby.

In the middle of this new life, Kirsa and I tied the knot in Holland, then returned home to five pages of shock-horror snatched photos in *¡Hola!* It was all splashed under a heading of *'boda sorpresa!'*, which meant 'surprise wedding!', and I thought, *what* fucking surprise? What was a surprise were the bloody photos. It went on to say that it was a *boda sorpresa* of *'Kirsa van Palland con el inglés, Timoty Porfitt'*. Jesus Christ, it was that fart-arse-Porfitt again! First 'Thimotty', now 'Timoty'! They couldn't even get my name right on my own wedding day. Everyone else looked perfect but I looked like a complete anorak. Kirsa looked stunning in her 'beautiful burgundy and cream dress, topped with a tall riding hat and veil'. But they described her as a 'beautiful ex-model', which made her cringe, because she'd never been one. They went on to describe her as being 'discreet, enjoys her privacy, and keeps herself to herself to look after her kids'. *Exactly* – so why the hell did they publish a load of photos snatched at her wedding?

'*No pasa nada,*' said Luis again, laughing it all off. He was curious to know how the photos came out, though, and I told him I had no idea but Kirsa had her suspicions.

'Anyway, my own daughter looks so *bella* in the photos, don't you think?' added Luis. 'And if you look closely, you'll see that it's *my* hand she's holding …'

Soon afterwards we moved out of the unpronounceable Povedilla 13 flat into a more spacious one, further outside the centre of Madrid, in San Martin de Porres. We had a communal garden and swimming pool there, and neighbours with kids the same ages as ours. I soon realised that when kids had other kids to play with, they were happier and got exhausted more quickly, too. I taught Adrian to swim and we now had proper lawns to kick a ball around, instead of having to walk over to the filthy Fuente del Berro park whilst dodging all the *Madrileño* dog pooh.

We moved our Barcelona office to smaller, cheaper premises on the Paseo de Gràcia. As we were so busy, my plan of flying backwards and forwards had started to go wrong. I asked the girls in Barcelona to find somewhere like my original Madrid *apartamento* in the Centro Colón. But instead of a greasy turquoise *apartamento*, Yolanda found me the sumptuous Hotel Arts in the Olympic port, forty-four storeys high with panoramic views on all sides over the city and Mediterranean. It didn't take us long to find ways that *Vogue* and the hotel could work together, and I virtually moved in during the weekdays, lock, stock and *banderilla*. Here, in a huge bath-robe, in my pastel-coloured penthouse-suite with marble bathrooms (yes, plural) on the thirty-something floor, if I wanted the Bang & Olufsen CD-player to open I simply clapped my hands. I'd never seen something so sophisticated – and I don't think Spain had, either. In fact we'd come along way, Spain and I, since the days of my crackling radio-cassette player in the Colón.

36

Flash forward. It is early 1996. Kirsa and I, together with my new Spanish *Vogue* editor, Mara Malibrán, are in Milan for the night, attending some fashion shows, and the Giorgio Armani show in particular. It is a far cry from the day I first walked into *Vogue* House, London, at the age of eighteen, and asked for a job – and only got one because I reminded the personnel manager of her nephew.

A lady called Isabel Preysler is with us. Isabel Preysler is the ex-wife of the ever-tanned Latin crooner, Julio Iglesias, whom she married when she was just nineteen. She is therefore the mum of heartthrob Enrique Iglesias. She is also the ex-wife of the Marqués de Gríñon, or Carlos Falcó, as he prefers to be called, the aristocratic non-conformist who just happens to grow some of the best grapes in Spain. Today, however, she is the wife of the ex-Finance Minister of Spain, Miguel Boyer, one of the country's most successful businessmen. Isabel Preysler is *¡Hola!* magazine's constant and loyal cover star, a close friend of King Juan Carlos and the Spanish royal family, as well as an integral part of Spanish high society. She is the PR-mafia's must-have guest at a never-ending social circuit where the Spanish glitterati of *empresarios*, singers, actors, writers, *toreros, futbolistas*, flamenco stars, designers, models and key social celebrities, all fight to rub Armani-clad shoulders with her. To me, she's just a great lady in a great dress. It just so happens that since she's also done an Armani shoot for us in *Vogue*, she's become a sort of friend. She's even hidden under the dashboard of my new Mercedes whilst I've smuggled her out of our office to avoid the *paparazzi*.

After his catwalk show, Giorgio Armani has invited us to his private quarters in the elegant *palacete* for a cocktail party before dinner. Among the guests are Sophia Loren, Claudia Cardinale, Martin Scorsese and Eric Clapton. An official *¡Hola!* photographer takes shots of Isabel with Giorgio, then Isabel with Sophia, then Isabel with Claudia, then Isabel with Giorgio, Sophia and Claudia altogether. I'm exhausted and could do with an early night back at the hotel (without any kids jumping on me in the morning), but I feel as if I am on the film-set of something which is too good to be missed. I eye Giorgio's private telephone next to Sophia Loren. It has already rung once or twice for one of the guests and I am tempted to phone my dad in England from it and yell, 'Hi, dad! Hang on a sec, I'm just going to pass you to Sophia Loren. Yes, *Sophia Loren!* No, the real one. Yes, the *real* Sophia Loren, dad!' I can see myself covering the mouthpiece with my palm, passing it to Sophia, saying, 'Just say, *"Ciao, Ronnie …"'*

Instead, I wander around the room, admiring the paintings and furniture, watching everyone else, and wondering what time we'll be able to leave. Suddenly this woman approaches me. She's an American, fairly tall, very, *very* thin, with wide eyes, a strange fixed grin, and taut stretched skin. She is watching Isabel being photographed and asks me if I know who she is.

'Sure, I do,' I reply. 'That's Isabel Preysler.'

'And that photographer?' asks the skeleton.

'I think he's with *¡Hola!,*' I say. 'I think they're doing an official shoot with her and Giorgio to cover his shows.'

She pauses, trying to take this all in.

'*¡Hola!?*' she finally spits. 'That's that *Spanish* magazine, right?'

'Right,' I nod, quietly wondering who's been rattling *her* cage.

She pauses again, then says sharply: 'I always see people *buying* it at airports.'

'Right,' I nod. She's said 'buying' as if it's a crime. What are people supposed to do? This woman is highly-strung and wacko, no doubt about it. Whoever she is, she's too rich, too thin and too irritating for me. 'Right,' I say again, trying to catch Kirsa's eye. 'Oh well, I suppose I'd better go and – '

'Why is it so popular?' continues the skeleton, abruptly.

'It's also very successful in England,' I say. 'It's called *Hello!* over there. And I reckon they'll launch a version in the States one day. Perhaps they could call it *Hi!*'

I start to laugh but she glares at me as if I'm demented.

'Oh, *really!*' she shrieks, as if I've just sprinted stark-bollock-naked across her lawn at the Hamptons. 'You really think something like that would work in the States? I mean, it's a European thing, isn't it – what with all your royal families?'

I turn to have a good look at her.

She's beginning to appear vaguely familiar but I still can't place her. She's glaring at me and by now, Kirsa has joined us, having overheard the last few lines of our conversation. 'Oh,' I say, oddly finding myself defending the *¡Hola!* philosophy more than it deserves. '*¡Hola!* and *Hello!* don't just publish pictures of royal families, you know. And anyway, even if you don't exactly have a royal family, you still have the Kennedys, Trumps and all that crap …'

There's a brief, deafening silence, before:

'Oh, my *Gawwwd!*' whines the skeleton, twisting her head and neck around in what looks like agony. '*Puh-lease* don't mention us both in the same sentence!'

'I'm sorry?' I say.

Kirsa whispers loudly in my ear.

'Tim,' she says. 'It's Jackie Kennedy's sister …'

'Oh, *right,*' I say, turning beetroot and wanting to hurl myself out of Giorgio Armani's window.

What was *I* even doing there? My love affair with Spain was never supposed to have turned out like this. I was sent to Madrid for six weeks *nine years ago,* for heaven's sake. I'd overstayed my welcome by nearly a decade.

Dear Luis. He'd invited me to Spain. He'd employed Kirsa. He'd certainly become my father figure in Spain, my mentor, my boss and my best friend. We were at home the day before my thirty-fourth birthday, at San Martin de Porres, our new flat in Puerto de Hierro, when Luis called. He chatted with Kirsa, who was now pregnant, asking her how she was feeling, how the other kids were, how I was, how everything was, before casually letting slip that he wasn't feeling well himself, and that he and Ana-María wouldn't be able to come to the lunch we were throwing the next day as he had to go for a check-up. It was the last time Kirsa would ever speak to him. Later that night, much later, his wife Ana-María called, in tears. Luis was in the Clínica Ruber and they feared he had leukaemia. She started to apologise about my birthday, but I told her that tomorrow was already cancelled.

I wanted to see Luis. When I arrived at the clinic

the next day, Giovanni was also there. We spent ages with Luis and then Giovanni came back to our flat for 'a cup of tea' afterwards. Kirsa and I sat with him and we all had tea and then I eventually poured him a whisky-*ito*, too, and he started to recount tales of his time in Brazil with Luis – how Luis once 'sold' him together with a gourmet magazine that he was off-loading to another publisher, and Luis only informed Giovanni when *El Principe* himself turned up for work as normal, and Luis said, 'No, Giovanni, I've *sold* you, you don't work here anymore, you need to go to another office.' And Kirsa and I laughed, and I poured Giovanni another whisky-*ito*, and then we all started to feel that it would all be OK. But it wasn't. The mood in the Sir Rhino Twes office the next day was very dark, and María-Teresa, Kirsa, Giovanni, José Luis, Rachele, and even Alonso, the dear old *chófer*, spent the day moping and waiting around with one another. The news, when it came, was bad.

The next day I got a call from Luis himself in the clinic and he tried to laugh a little, telling me that the latest gossip was that our finance director was unhappy that Jonathan Newhouse had asked *me* to collect him from the airport when he flew in the next day. He added something I'll never forget which was: 'This is the type of thing that *you're* going to have to handle from now on.' Giovanni and I saw Luis again on the Sunday, with Giovanni coming back for tea and a couple of whisky-*itos* again.

When I approached María Teresa's desk first thing

Wednesday, I saw her in floods of tears. As the news filtered round the office that Luis had died, staff cut short their telephone conversations and stopped tapping away at their typewriters, until all you could hear was muffled sobbing. Like others, I was distraught, utterly drained. All I could think of was that Luis had gone, wasn't going to see the birth of our baby, and that I was going to ask him to be godfather.

That same evening, we all paid our last respects at the sombre *velatorio* wake. I'd never seen a dead body before. As I gazed through the glass at Luis's corpse, I didn't recognise it as the Luis I knew. Luis was still *here*, as far as I was concerned. His voice, eyes, smile, warmth and generosity were still in the air. He was fifty-eight.

Jonathan was also very distressed and moved into the Hotel Palace for a couple of nights. The next day, he sat in Luis's office to sort out numerous matters, yet also worked his way through calling all the directors in one by one throughout the day. I was called in last and found Jonathan sitting in the chair opposite where Luis used to sit, which was his normal position whenever the three of us had our monthly meetings together. I pulled up and sat in the chair alongside him – diagonally – also my normal place, and so we were both sitting there as if Luis was still chairing the meeting, but his absence and spirit seemed to fill his empty chair more than if he was physically sitting in it himself. I knew Jonathan could feel this, too – because he kept glancing over at 'Luis', and when we started our conversation about our shared grief at the loss of our friend, we both found ourselves glancing at the empty chair.

Then Jonathan suddenly asked me what I would do if I were to take Luis's job, and how I saw the company developing. The question took me by surprise, but what surprised me even more was how easy I found it to reply. Easy, because I felt Luis was sitting there beside me, checking that I was telling Jonathan everything that I needed to tell him. I spoke at length, answering more points, until eventually it seemed that he'd asked all the questions he needed to ask. Except for one.

'Oh, sorry, there *is* one final thing,' he said. 'Is it true that when you were at Condé Nast in London, you tried to fuck anything that was blonde and wearing a skirt?'

'Who said that?' I said, genuinely stunned.

'Annie Holcroft,' he said, very calmly and still with a straight face. Annie Holcroft was the Publishing Director of *Tatler* and *Vanity Fair*.

'Oh,' I said, still stunned. 'Well, I didn't dare try anything on with her.'

There was a pause while he tried to digest this. Then: 'Great!' he said, finally laughing and clapping his hands together as if they were cymbals. 'Well, this has been a very interesting, constructive, enjoyable meeting. Thank you very much.'

We shook hands again and I made to leave the room, with a final glance at 'Luis' in his empty chair.

A week later, Jonathan was back in Madrid again.

We were all due to attend a mass memorial service for Luis that evening. As soon as he arrived, I was called by María Teresa to go and see him. He stood up to greet me, shaking my hand and closing the door, then quickly took out a single sheet of paper from his briefcase, before handing it to me with the words, 'Just check it's OK, will you?'

I scanned the first line. It was an internal memo, and it started, 'I am pleased to announce the appointment of Tim Parfitt as managing director of Condé Nast in Spain.' I inhaled sharply but read on, down to the last paragraph, where Jonathan's words included, 'When Luis was alive, he and I often talked about the future of Condé Nast in Spain. Luis considered Tim to be his protégé and the correct person to succeed him …' Then when I finally got to the end, I looked up to see Jonathan grinning and savouring my reaction.

'I don't know what to say,' I said. 'Thank you, Jonathan. Really.'

I left the office quietly and told no-one except Kirsa. We hardly spoke later on, standing side by side in church during the memorial service with what seemed like the entire population of Madrid – old, young and intimate friends of Luis, all past and current employees, contributors, clients, acquaintances, anyone it seemed he had ever once met.

Afterwards, Jonathan beckoned us to get into the back of the Jag with him. We dropped him at the Hotel Palace and, when he'd gone, I pulled off my black mourning tie and got in the front seat alongside

Alonso, squeezing his arm as he started to purr the Jag back down to the Paseo del Prado and then along towards Cibeles. We got out halfway along Recoletos and I dragged Kirsa across the road and into the beautiful Espejo café where much of all this began – and where I now sat clutching a cold tumbler of beer as Kirsa clutched *me* – and where the cross-eyed barman, if he could see me, would have seen tears rolling down my cheeks.

37

It was going to be fun, though. It was a sad way to inherit a job, but even Luis would admit that it was going to be fun. Fun but difficult. I was going to continue to put myself through a minor hell, albeit a delicious and glamorous one, as things needed to change in the company. I was going to have to restructure, modernise, computerise and relocate us, change *Vogue* editors, launch *GQ*, hire, fire and 'retire' – all in this language that they called Spanish and which I *still* didn't really have a good grasp of.

'How old *is* Alonso?' Jonathan telephoned to ask me one day, early on.

'I don't know,' I tried to joke. 'Eighty? Ninety? He's getting on.'

'Seriously.'

'Jonathan, I have absolutely no idea. Why do you ask?'

'Well, look,' he said, 'put it this way. I want you to

send Alonso for a check-up before he collects Si from the airport this time round ...'

'You *what?*' I said. 'How the hell am I going to get him to do that?'

'I don't care,' said Jonathan. 'But I want him checked over. The whole works. Are you certain he's not even past the insurance age?'

Poor Alonso.

Collecting our multi-billionaire proprietor, Si Newhouse, from the airport had become an annual treat for him, and you couldn't retire someone like Alonso, you just couldn't. We did try, though – several times, in fact – and we even had a mass collection for him, and bought him a beautiful watch and threw a farewell drinks party after work, with Giovanni making a speech – but then he was back the next day, first thing, standing next to Sylvia's desk and asking for his instructions. I don't know what it was, but maybe he didn't understand the way I said 'retire' in Spanish. *'Vamos a jubilarte, Alonso,'* I'd say – 'We're going to retire you, Alonso,' – but maybe he thought *'jubilarte'* was a street in Madrid or something, because he always seemed to excitedly get out his *A-Z* and scan the index whenever I announced this. So we gave up, and Alonso was still with us, and always would be, even though Jonathan finally banned him from picking up Si from the airport again.

Though we'd met a few times, I'd never really got to know Si Newhouse at all. A month after I took over, however, mid-May 94, he flew in with Jonathan.

Instead of Casa Lucio, I took them for dinner at the Ritz where they were staying. Because we were in the middle of the *fiesta* of San Isidro, I made some polite conversation about the bullfight festival, when Si suddenly announced that he used to love bullfights many years ago, and that he would love to go again if I'd take him. This came as a big surprise to Jonathan. We all quickly agreed that it would have to be *next* year, when he visited again during May. But he didn't let the conversation drop away from bullfights at all, and started going on about all the Hemingway that he'd read and loved. I mentioned *The Dangerous Summer*, all about the rivalry between Ordóñez and Dominguín, and he said that he hadn't read that one but would like to. I told him I'd lend him my copy (which I did). We just seemed to hit it off, Si and I, chatting away happily about the *corrida* most of the evening, sipping our iced wine in the elegant restaurant of the Ritz.

The next year, when Jonathan and Si's private plane touched down at Barajas airport at five in the afternoon on 31 May, in the middle of San Isidro, I was still in the office, waiting anxiously for news from Alonso himself, who had been busy for over a month trying to secure four of the best seats for that evening's seven o'clock *corrida*.

In fact Alfonso had gone over the top and secured the very best seats in the house, getting us four front-row *barreras* in the shaded *sombra* just behind where the matadors draped their capes, and for one of the best bullfights in the festival with Ortega Cano, 'Joselito' and 'Finito de Cordoba'. He'd paid – or at least he *said* he'd paid – the *peseta* equivalent of 500 quid for the four, but he'd *delivered*, that was the main thing, and Si and Jonathan were going to love it.

But just before we were supposed to pick them up at the Ritz, Jonathan called. There'd been a change of plan – *a change of plan?* – and that instead of the bullfight, they'd decided that they were just going for a gentle jog in the Retiro ...

'A gentle *fucking* jog?' I yelled. 'What the hell's *that?*'

We used up the 500 quid tickets by taking Sylvia and Alicia, one of the editorial secretaries, to sit in the front row of Las Ventas for one of the top bullfights of the season, sitting a few spaces away from the King of Spain.

Toby James Parfitt van Pallandt arrived appropriately on 7 July 1994, the patron saint's day of Pamplona, the San Fermin of Hemingway fame. It was an especially stifling summer, far too hot to be spending the night trying to sleep on a white plastic sofa in the airless Clinica Nuevo Parque, only to slide off it first thing in the morning, so slippery had it become with sweat. Nevertheless, I have never known such a feeling of total happiness and completeness. I was so in love with my new son and my beautiful wife and family.

The *paparazzi* were outside and Toby's very first experience of fresh air and daylight was then ruined by the ridiculous amount of flashbulbs hovering over him as I wrestled him out of the clinic, arm in arm with Kirsa and into the back seat of the waiting Mercedes with Alonso sitting proudly at the wheel. Then the blurred and very first photo of him in *¡Hola!* – hardly a day old – was accompanied by a caption re-christening him, of course, as Toby 'Jones Porfitt', and weighing him in at just 2.3 kg, as opposed to his very respectable 3.2 kg. I faxed what I believed to be an angry note to the magazine, complaining that it was a crime to rob my son of so much weight at such an early age. The owner himself called minutes later to apologise.

A new baby inevitably meant new vocabulary, which soon included nipple-pads, too, which Kirsa urgently sent me out to purchase one day, from the Mothercare-style shop, Prenatal.

'Do you have nipples like pillows?' I managed in my still dreadful Spanish. '*Tienes almohadillas como pezónes?*'

'*Cómo?*' exclaimed the shop assistant.

I tried twiddling my own nipples through my T-shirt as I tried to explain that what I *really* needed were some nipple cushions to stop myself from leaking milk.

38

Soon after I'd taken over from Luis – and soon after Toby's birth – Kirsa and I had moved our expanding family into a large rented house called Monte Alto, in Humera, just outside Madrid. Hidden among pine trees, it was a glorious, whitewashed, rustic, *finca*-style sprawl with open-fireplaces, numerous lawns, and a large swimming pool. At last we'd moved into a little paradise, a slice of Spain I'd spent seven years searching for.

The amazing Nelci, our kids' new nanny, also moved in with us, which allowed Kirsa the time to return to work, and we were also soon joined by Barnaby, an over-affectionate, black puppy retriever, who arrived as a present from Luis's widow and Toby's godmother, Ana-María. As we had been encouraged to follow Luis's path and entertain clients and 'Condé Nast friends' at home, Jonathan agreed to pay the rent on the new house. It was at Monte Alto, therefore, that I would throw a party to celebrate the launch of our Spanish *GQ*. It was at Monte Alto that I would eventually throw a huge party for the Spanish fashion industry. It was at Monte Alto where Giovanni continued to visit us every Sunday afternoon for 'tea' followed by a whisky-*ito* or two, as indeed he had done ever since the weekend that we last saw Luis alive. It was from Monte Alto that we would all stroll down to christen Toby in the tiny Humera church, with Giovanni escorting my mother, arm-in-arm, and with Clem turning up late, as always. It was at Monte Alto where the kids would play in the garden for hours on end with Barnaby and their friends, and Luis's children, María-Duarte and Pedro, now part of our extended family. It was while at Monte Alto that Clara would enrol in the neighbouring riding school eventually to come second in the Spanish junior dressage championships. It was at Monte Alto, too, that I finally learnt how to pronounce Spanish ...

To keep us both in trim, Barnaby and I would go running in the vast Casa de Campo, adjacent to the house. Well, actually, *Barnaby* would run and I would cycle.

One day, I was cycling happily along, thinking about the things I *loathed* about Spain. There weren't many. A lack of pet shops, was one. The way Spaniards *drove* was another. The way they rode motor-bikes with their crash helmets hooked through their *arms*, too, or the way they balanced their poor kids on the handlebars. I hated the fact that they never looked behind, as well. They never looked in the mirror when they were driving and they never looked behind when they were strolling along. The worst, of course, was whenever you followed any Spaniard on an escalator, only to pile in to them at the end, because they would just stop and stand there, totally oblivious to you coming up behind. In fact there was something about Spaniards not ever wanting to be alone that irritated me, too. Sit on an empty beach in Spain and a Spaniard will come and put his towel down right beside you, smoking.

And then a bee stung me on the lip.

It was definitely a bee. I could feel and *see* my own face starting to swell up. Even the dog started to give me funny looks as we made our way back home on the quickest track possible. After sleeping with a wine-cooler on it, I looked like a botoxed Elephant Man in the morning, with the swelling having manoeuvred, expanded and stretched itself over the entire left hand side of my face.

There was no other option but to visit the nearest doctor, a tiny, brand new clinic in the nearby suburb of Pozuelo.

I was ushered through for a consultation with what looked and sounded like a Scottish-Spaniard. Vocally ginger, visually Mediterranean, he'd obviously learnt his English at a Glaswegian medical college. He barely looked up at me, not even to greet me.

'So, *Señor Parfeee* …' he purred. 'What brings you to Madrid?'

'Uh-huh,' I mumbled. I could hardly speak, my face was so swollen.

'Oh, really? That sounds exciting.'

'Huh-huh.'

'And what is it you actually *do* for them?' He was scribbling notes, still not having really looked at me.

'Huh-huh, huh-huh.'

'Oh, really? That sounds exciting. How long have you been here?'

'Uh-huh-ughhhh!'

'Oh, really? That sounds exciting.'

Then he finished scribbling and looked up.

'So what can I do for you, then?'

'Uh-huh!' I moaned, pointing at my face.

'I'm sorry, *Señor Parfeeee* – could you possibly just repeat that?'

'Duh yuh thuh-ink I look lark thith all thur farking time?' I shouted.

'Well,' he said, finally peering closer at me. 'We get all sorts in here, you know, *Señor Parfeeee* ... ' Then: 'Oh sweet Mary Mother of Jesus! What the bloody hell's happened to your face?'

And then it happened.

Because my face was so swollen, I suddenly amazed both myself *and* the ginger Spaniard. I found I could pronounce the Spanish word for bee, *abejorro*, absolutely perfectly.

'Arf bin thtung by a farking *ah-be-horro!*' I barked.

So I now had fluent Spanish, too.

Additional Chapters

39

The day that Jonathan announced my appointment to run the Spanish company, we'd sat alone for a while in Luis's office.

He congratulated me again, shaking my hand, and then we sort of patted one another. We spoke about many things. About how we'd work together, about my new terms, and about how the others might react to my appointment, with Jonathan pointing out that there might be a problem with one specific director, but that all the others had spoken very highly of me when he'd had his one-to-ones with the key staff.

Then I said something that was to later prove quite important: 'I guess this means Kirsa should now leave the company.'

Jonathan shook his head. He said that it wouldn't be a problem at all. On the contrary, she'd be an 'asset', he said. He went on to say that I had a lot on my plate, though – that inheriting the job in such circumstances would not be easy – 'You also have a baby on the way, remember?' – and that I was 'only thirty-four' with a lot of things happening in my life all at once, but he was in no doubt that I could handle it.

I was in no doubt, too.

I moved Mara Malibrán, our deputy editor of *Vogue*, over to edit *GQ* and to implement my blueprint for the magazine. Once we launched successfully in November 1994, I received a note from Jonathan that said, 'The premier issue of *GQ* is outstanding, one of the best first issues of a magazine I have ever seen' – which was a good start. Then Si Newhouse himself faxed over a short note, simply saying: 'Congratulations on Spanish *GQ*. It looks great.' No mention of bullfights, either.

Rachele Enriquez, our editor of Spanish *Vogue*, had been furious with me for stealing Mara to edit the men's title, though – and I probably showed early signs of my lack of tact (at least in comparison to Luis) when I snapped back, telling her that I didn't need to ask her permission for anything.

Our constant spats continued during meetings to discuss editorial page allocations and the overall look of the magazine. My instructions from Jonathan had been to modernise and grow the company, and that was to also include a long-overdue redesign and facelift of *Vogue* itself. While it was no secret that Rachele was keen to move back to her home in Milan, it was a matter of when and how that would be done, seamlessly and elegantly so – and, more importantly, who I would choose to replace her.

Editing *Vogue* is the top job for all aspiring fashion hacks, and the rumours were already circling among the Spanish *moda*-mafia that Rachele's days in Madrid were numbered – which meant that discreet approaches from potential successors started to filter through from all our competitor titles and beyond.

Sylvia (who now had a desk alongside María Teresa) marked a series of secret lunch meetings for me with a few candidates, and I spent long periods analysing our magazine with each one to see if they had the same vision for it as I did. I wanted to make it bolder, louder and livelier, and even inject touches of humour into it, like British *Vogue*. In the end, I opted for Mara herself, who I'd only just moved across to *GQ*, but where she'd understood what I wanted and had done a great job. Once she'd edited three issues of *GQ*, I moved her back in preparation to take over the editorship of *Vogue*, with Rachele's imminent return to Italy. Meanwhile, 'Sandra of the River' arrived to replace Mara on our men's title …

Sandra del Rio joined us in mid-February 1995. She was always great fun with a big smile and a mischievous wink, but the problem I had with her was that she couldn't get enough *'sexo'* …

Sandra had her own vocabulary when it came to

the magazine's cover lines. This meant that she tried to literally sex up every Spanish word she could. So '*excesivo*', for example, became '*SEXcesivo*' with Sandra, and '*extra*' became '*SEXtra*', and you could never be just ecstatic about something, it was *SEXtático*. Everything was a SEXaggeration, followed by not just one SEXclamation mark, but two!! – and sometimes even *twes*!!!

The *GQ* cover meetings were often bizarre, therefore, with Sandra trying to use as many '*sexo*' cover lines as possible, or at least cover lines that screamed: 'I'm SEXY! Buy Me!'

Condé Nast International had initiated studies across all its titles to try and see what celebrities, models, cover lines or even just colours, sold better than others – and in the case of *GQ*, the early signs from London seemed to point in a rather obvious direction: Naomi Campbell's naked buttocks, gently sprinkled with wet sand, sold ten times more copies than an image of Prince Charles.

It didn't take us long to follow suit in Spain. Harrison Ford had appeared on the first cover of Spanish *GQ* – and sales were great but helped by the fact that it was a launch.

Issue two was Anthony Hopkins and the sales weren't hot. Issue three had Liz Hurley's left breast jutting out of a safety-pin dress and the sales were good; we should have learnt from it. Issue four was Harvey Keitel. It was Sandra's first issue and her *Pulp Fiction* cover. She should have chosen Uma Thurman instead, but she didn't listen to me. The result? Crap sales.

Issue five and she did listen to me. It was a *'rubias'* (blondes) themed cover, with Sharon Stone sitting provocatively on the edge of a bed, wearing a black negligee with the strap hanging off her shoulder. The result? Our sales shot through the roof. So, with issue six, we went the whole way with supermodel Helena Christensen's nipples ...

We'd been sold the stunning images of Helena Christensen by the late, Illinois-born editor of British *GQ*, Michael VerMuelen. He'd had great fun with them himself, and would then boast about it on the phone to me – all about how he'd accompanied one image with the cover line: 'Seriously, would you leave *this* for Paula Yates?'

When his magazine hit the streets, he told me that the INXS singer Michael Hutchence (who *had* left Christensen for Yates), telephoned him and went ballistic. VerMuelen did a 'call back' to check the number, then phoned *The Sun* newsdesk and asked them to ring Hutchence immediately to ask for his view about the latest *GQ*. It meant the issue was a sell-out, at least that's what Michael V told me ...

But it wasn't just the personality, or the state of undress of the personality on the cover, that was important. The cover lines were crucial, too. Our research told us that the bestselling covers tended to include not only a 'sexclamation' mark or two, but also a number and a question mark. So, '50 ways to do something' always worked well, as did a question, such as, 'Are you getting enough?' The words 'official' and 'survey' worked well, too – as well as the words, and preferably always in capitals: SEX (of course), HOT, NEW, INSIDE, FREE, A-Z and EXCLUSIVE.

Sandra would try and cram all the words into the same sentence, then strut excitedly into my office with a mock-up of the cover. I'd take one look at it and see something that contained the equivalent words in Spanish of, 'SEXCLUSIVE FREE A-Z SURVEY INSIDE!!! WHAT ARE THE 50 HOT NEW SEXERCISES TO KEEP YOUR GIRL BEGGING FOR MORE?'

'For fucksake, Sandra, we're not *Cosmopolitan*,' I'd cry, and she'd look at me as if I'd broken her heart.

We even had monthly *sexo* columns in both our magazines, written by Anka Radakovich for *Vogue*, and an utterly unpronounceable sexologist for *GQ*, called ... *wait for it ...*

José Ramón Landarroitajáuregui.

'Who the hell is Ho-Say Wamon Land-A-Wroita-Jerry-Kerry?' I'd say, once I'd seen the magazine's new contents page.

And María Teresa would wet herself again.

40

With Condé Nast covering the entire rent of our house in Humera, it meant we could also afford to send Adrian to the American School of Madrid in nearby Pozuelo. It opened my eyes to the fact that we were now living quite a luxurious 'ex-pat' lifestyle – a far cry from the bed that folded down from the greasy turquoise wall in my Centro Colón *apartamento*.

At the co-educational American school with its baseball diamond, cheerleading and visiting NASA astronauts giving talks, Adrian was even awarded a Great Turkey Certificate for helping to prepare a Thanksgiving feast. We started to get inundated with Parent Teacher Association newsletters and 'International Newcomers Club' invites and requests – even though we weren't really newcomers. All the bumph would arrive home in his homework-bag every week, containing all the latest fun and games for the thriving *guiri* community.

A Load of Bull

I often wondered how many ex-pat parents found the time to do the jobs they'd been sent over to do, what with all the volunteering, baking, sewing, face-painting, costume and prop-making that some international schools obliged them to do. But I guess it was comforting to know that if we ever had to leave Spain in a hurry, there were also 'International Support Staff' who'd come over and empty our fridge-freezer and aquarium ... if we had one.

There was even a shop in Pozuelo for *guiris* called *Smith's*. Hidden among the jars of Branston Pickle and boxes of Shredded Wheat, you could also find root beer, Reese's peanut butter bars and maple syrup. 'Satellite problem? No problem!' promised *Smith's* – and so we also invested in a satellite dish, meaning we could crash out in front of the OJ Simpson trial or the Jay Leno Show, whenever I wasn't client-entertaining – while the kids had *The Simpsons*. Adrian's best friend was the son of a US Army Sergeant, and together with other kids they all appeared in our *Vogue Niños* kids' supplement, making brownies with Giovanni and using ingredients from *Smith's* ... which I later helped to eat, of course.

Indeed, I should have perhaps joined the 'IOA', the International Overeaters Anonymous, which I saw advertised in one of the newcomers' newsletters ...

Sylvia filled my diary with delicious yet fattening client lunches that took in the best restaurants of Madrid, with my favourites being *El Amparo* in Puigcerdá, *Cabo Mayor* in Juan Ramón Jiménez, and the *Mesón Txistu* Basque steak-house in the Plaza Ángel Carvajo – not far from the Bernabeu stadium and frequented by Real Madrid players. I often longed for simple *tapas* in the *Espejo*, however, or a good old debauched night in the Sevillana club *Almonte* – instead of hosting Fragrance Awards at The Ritz, or attending countless cocktail-*itos* at embassies, shop openings and product launches.

In between all the eating and entertaining, the job was hard, and there was much to do …

I did what Jonathan asked me to do. I modernised the company. I increased our magazines' sales and advertising share. I cut some costs. I overhauled several departments, recruiting new sales, marketing, production and circulation managers – all efficient, bilingual and energetic. With our new, dynamic commercial director, it wasn't long before we had special promotions, 'advertorials' and supplements lined up to pitch to clients for six months ahead at a time. Kirsa was back full-time, too, working on our new *Vogue Novias* bridal magazine with Ana María, Luis's widow. The communication between all departments, especially between Madrid and Barcelona, had never been better. Along the way, we also replaced our finance director, as Jonathan had lost confidence in him.

We needed new premises, too. *Sir Rhino Twes* had become cramped. We'd filled it with too many glass partitions to create numerous cubby-hole offices, and we simply didn't fit into the old place anymore. As we also had to get computerised and 'networked' (we were already behind the times), we needed a modern office already set up with underfloor cabling – and it would have cost a fortune to rip up the old, creaky wooden floors at *Sir Rhino*.

In my search for suitably elegant premises, I involved Giovanni, as he'd know if an address was good or not. We finally found the perfect office space – modern, but renovated from an old *palacete* – in the Paseo de Castellana, 9-11 – and yes, much easier to pronounce. On one of Si's visits, we took him there with Jonathan to show him the space we planned to occupy, which was only *half* the floor. He said, 'Take the *whole* floor, what with all your expansion plans ...'

We moved in at the end of August 1995, fully computerised, following countless internal discussions and squabbles as to who would occupy what space. I didn't realise, of course, that I would personally last just seven months in the new offices that I'd carefully designed myself ...

41

Jonathan was in Madrid at least once a month to start with, no doubt to help ease me into my new role. He'd arrive in time for a dinner somewhere, then we'd spend the following day in the office, and then sometimes he'd stay an extra night if there was an event to take him along to. I enjoyed his visits because I enjoyed his company, and I always believed the feeling was mutual.

On one occasion, he arrived with a brand new edition of French *Vogue* under his arm – the first edition from a new editor in Paris. Instead of discussing how our Spanish company was doing for the first half-hour or so, he asked me to flick through the French magazine, page by page, and give my views on it. When I asked why, he said he really admired how I could analyse and dissect a magazine. I thought that was a great compliment from the owner of a magazine empire such as Condé Nast. In fact, it reminded me of our first ever meeting, analysing *Casa Vogue*, when I'd told him it was crap. But sometimes I could never tell if Jonathan heard everything I said, or whether he took on board all my comments.

I once told him that he should look at an early edition of a new British magazine called *FHM* that I'd picked up at an airport. I told him that it was 'clever' and that it looked livelier and smarter than British *GQ* (*and* our Spanish *GQ*). He didn't seem to be listening, so I insisted: 'Believe me, Jonathan, *FHM* will go far.' A week or so later, I suddenly got a call from Nick Coleridge, my counterpart at Condé Nast in London, jovially saying, 'Jonathan tells me you were praising *FHM* and that we should watch it carefully,' – although I could tell that he wanted me, in future, to mind my own bloody business.

The fact that Jonathan *did*, therefore, take on board my comments about other magazines, made it even more surprising that we were to eventually fall out over my opinion of our own magazine: Spanish *Vogue*.

Jonathan even came to Madrid a few times with his new wife, Ronnie Cooke – a friendly enough, former founding-employee of *Details* magazine in the States (where I think she first met Jonathan).

Kirsa and I had dinner with them several times – and even dragged them along to our fourth annual *Vogue* polo tournament, which was a great success. Then Jonathan and Ronnie came round to our house for a leisurely lunch the day after the polo, and Jonathan went jogging and swam in the pool with the kids. As always, he was good company. And as always, I never expected anything would go wrong …

I was twenty-seven when I was sent to Madrid for just six weeks to help launch Spanish *Vogue*. I was now thirty-five and had been running the company for nearly two years.

I had a great salary. We were living rent-free in one of the most exclusive areas just outside Madrid. The kids were at private school and we had a live-in nanny for our new son. The job was tough, stressful but also glamorous, and in one of the most amazing cities in the world. I had a top-of-the-range Mercedes-Benz and even a chauffeur when I wanted one … only because Alonso had still refused to retire.

Life was great.

But then it all went wrong.

42

During the last phase of Rachele's editorship of *Vogue*, and even more so once Mara had taken over, I threw myself into our next mission of improving the title, which also involved getting discreet feedback from top clients, fashion designers and some key executives I trusted at various ad agencies. I escorted my editors to the Versace, Chanel and Armani catwalk shows in Milan and Paris, but I often felt like an uninvited extra in *Prêt-à-Porter*, a film directed by Robert Altman that had just been released in Europe. Movies about the fashion world rarely work, however, because the truth is more *loco* than fiction. This 'glamorous' job was also a surreal world of ice queen fashionistas, a circus of superficial air-kissing, bitchy tantrums and backstabbing. I didn't feel it was my world, and it wasn't. *Magazines* were my world. *Publishing* was my world.

True to the flirtatious *Teeem Parfeee* who first arrived in Madrid, I even tried to 'chat up' the model Carla

Bruni backstage in Paris ... only because Mara introduced us.

'When are you coming to Madrid?' I asked.

'When are you going to put me on the cover of Spanish *Vogue*?' she said.

I just drooled an inane reply.

Later that night, I heard rumours that she was out on the town with Mick Jagger. Meanwhile, chubby me – tubby Timmy – well, I was tucked up in bed at my hotel.

Rachele edited Spanish *Vogue* up to and including the April 1995 issue, and then Mara took over.

When a *Vogue* editor changes, there are many casualties along the way. Out went most of Rachele's old team, and in came a new *'subdirector de moda'* and a strengthened team of *'estilistas'*. There were new sub-editors and a style editor lined up, too, and then our art director, Francisco Rodríguez, who'd been hanging in there ever since I first arrived, also decided to leave, which meant we had to find a replacement ...

Our new art director was American and a close friend of Jonathan's – or rather, a close friend of his wife's, I think, as they all once worked on a magazine in New York together.

Condé Nast belongs to the Newhouse family and if a Newhouse suggests that you see someone with the possibility of giving them a job – it's not easy to say no. The fact is that Spanish *Vogue* needed a redesign, and the new art director, originally from LA, seemed to be the right person to take on the role.

Mara, however, hated the idea – at least initially. She was distraught. She was permanently storming into my office in tears. She'd only just taken over the magazine and didn't want to be told by me, *or* Jonathan, *who* she had to choose as an art director – and especially not another non-Spanish-speaking *guiri*.

I should have listened to her, which I did, but I should have then defended her right to make her own choice, which I didn't. Everything would be fine, I assured her. But it wasn't, and in the back of mind I probably knew that it never would be ...

To Jonathan's credit, he did try and keep out of involving himself too much in whether the new art director was settling in or not – although there were the odd occasions when he did, which concerned me.

He called me out of the blue from Paris one day, sounding rather embarrassed, but asking if I could speed up some of the expenses that she was waiting to reclaim. I did, which infuriated my new finance director. I was also asked to check if I could hurry along whoever was taking their time to get her work or residential permits in order – which was fine. The most irritating of all, however, was to check if her work space in our new offices was going to be suitable. I had specifically only worked on the allocation of the new office space with a select number of directors, but the new art director stormed into my office once, furious because she'd heard there wouldn't be any natural light in her department. I told her it was untrue and, as politely as I could, to also keep the hell out of it. A few days later, on a call with Jonathan regarding other business, he ended the conversation with: 'The art department *will* have natural light in the new offices, won't it?'

Everything was okay for about a year, but then we finally fell out over a cover choice. Mara and her new art director, who'd finally bonded, chose a cover image that I thought looked naff – and I criticised it. It wasn't just the cover. The magazine was looking cheap, and our sales were flat. The fashion images and many layouts were poor, in my eyes – but it didn't matter what I thought anymore. I was later told that Kirsa had also been overheard criticising the latest edition. She probably shouldn't have, but she had good taste.

Early January 1996, Jonathan faxed over a note to congratulate Mara, with a copy to me, on the January issue of *Vogue*, which he described as 'excellent', 'visually compelling' and the best he'd seen from Spain.
　I disagreed.
　Two months later, I was sacked.

43

On Thursday 14 March 1996, nearly two years since the death of Luis, I had dinner in Paris on Jonathan's invitation. It wasn't just him and me, though. No, it was another one of his pan-European 'fashion dinner' get-togethers for Condé Nast Europe's 'elite' – or at least, the supposed 'elite' – the *Vogue* editors, fashion directors and 'us', the managing directors, although Nick in London was able to avoid it by coming up with the perfect excuse that his wife was about to give birth. He was best out of it.

The last time we'd all done this, I'd been squashed on a tiny table opposite Gianfranco Ferré, while Kirsa had much more fun on a table with Jean Paul Gaultier. She wasn't in Paris tonight, though. Jonathan had reminded me once or twice that I was to come on my own – so I knew something was up. I also knew something was up because after the catwalk show earlier in the evening for John Galliano – when we were all going backstage to congratulate the designer – I'd caught the eye of Jonathan's wife, who seemed uncomfortable on seeing me. I even caught sight of her nudging her husband, almost as if she was demanding that he should do something about me, there and then. Being Jonathan, he did. He came over and greeted me profusely, as if nothing was wrong.

He acted as if nothing was wrong at the dinner, too. In fact, he was on great form, slapping me on the back and telling me that he'd put me on the best table alongside the star designer himself, John Galliano – although in hindsight, I don't know why.

On Saturday at noon, unsure what to expect, I arrived at Jonathan's elegant hotel suite in Paris. We drank water and nibbled at a spread of sandwiches that had been prepared. He seemed uncomfortable. It certainly wasn't the Jonathan I knew. We talked about the latest *Vogue*. He said he'd heard that I wasn't happy with it 'again', that I didn't like a lot of the layouts or the fashion, and so he asked me to go through it with him. I did. I pointed out everything I didn't like, and explained why. This time he didn't agree with me. It was as simple as that.

'Tim,' he then said. 'Are you happy in Spain?'

'Yes, of course.'

'It's just that you mentioned that you might want to move back to England.'

'One day, perhaps. But I love Spain.'

'Are you sure? Because we could always look at something somewhere –'

'I love Spain.'

'– if you're not happy.'

'I love Spain.'

'Okay, well, I'm just checking.'

Then there was another one of those Jonathan silences again, but I knew he wasn't finished. There was still something on his mind that he needed to ask me. It was as if he was embarrassed to have to do so, but eventually it came.

'Tim, there *is* something else …'

'Yes?'

'I think Kirsa should leave the company.'

'I'm sorry?'

'I think Kirsa should perhaps leave the company.'

I didn't say anything for a few seconds, then I just said: 'That's fine.'

'It's just that –'

'It's fine, Jonathan,' I said. 'You don't need to explain.'

There was a pause.

'Jonathan,' I then said. 'When I took on the job two years ago, I suggested that it might have been better for her to leave the company –'

'I know –'

'And you said no, that she would be an asset –'

'I know,' he said, 'but maybe you were right.'

'Okay, but just as long as you know that I did once suggest it myself.'

There was another pause.

'How do you want to do it?' he asked. 'Do you want me to talk to her?'

'No, I'll do it,' I said.

As I left his hotel suite, I decided to spring a question on him.

'Jonathan, is my job safe?'

'Your job is safe,' he said. 'Don't be paranoid.'

I took Kirsa out to dinner in Pozuelo after I arrived back in Madrid that night, and I told her. I then went to the restaurant loo and threw up. It was gut-wrenching – and she had been really enjoying her job.

Jonathan once told me how to fire someone. He said the best way was to go to their office to do it, then you could always leave. So I knew what was happening on that Wednesday, 20 March, when on my way to work I received a phone call in the car from my commercial director, to tell me that Jonathan had arrived in Madrid and was sitting in my office ... just waiting for me.

'I'm sorry how this worked out,' he said, looking genuinely fed up with everything and shaking my hand, when we finally met again two days later, and after my lawyer and a representative of Jonathan's had left the meeting room.

'It's okay.'

'I want you to know something, though,' he said. 'I don't discard the idea that we might work together again.'

I didn't reply.

'I mean it,' he said.

I assumed they were just shallow words to soothe my exit, something he said to everyone, although he genuinely still looked embarrassed that he'd sacked me … or perhaps he'd been pushed into sacking me.

What he'd said was curious, though, because when I'd called my father in England last night to tell him about my dismissal, he'd listened carefully and then said: 'They'll ask you back one day.'

'No way.'

'They *will*,' he said. 'They'll ask you back one day.'

The greatest sadness of my life is that he wasn't around to witness it. He died two months later. His death drove me back to England to be with my mother, family and friends.

Just three years later, in early 1999, I got into the back of Jonathan's chauffeur-driven car outside Vogue House in London, and we went for lunch.

'I told you we'd work together again,' he said, slapping my knee.

About the Author

Tim Parfitt has worked in the media in London, Madrid and Barcelona, predominantly for Condé Nast, where he ran the Spanish company, helping to launch *Vogue España* and eventually launching *GQ* in Spain, among other titles. He later also worked for the Press Association, *La Vanguardia* and Grupo Planeta, editing, publishing, launching and re-launching titles as diverse as *Lonely Planet* and *Playboy*.

A Load of Bull – An Englishman's Adventures in Madrid was first published by Pan Macmillan in the UK. It was published in Spain by Almuzara under the title, *Mucho toro – las tribulaciones de un inglés en la movida*.

Tim's latest book, *The Barcelona Connection*, a crime-thriller sprinkled with black comedy, was published in April 2023.

Tim lives near Barcelona. He can be found at www.timothyparfitt.com and also writes on Substack at timparfitt.substack.com

Also by Tim Parfitt

The Barcelona Connection

www.ingramcontent.com/pod-product-compliance
Lightning Source LLC
Chambersburg PA
CBHW030545080526
44585CB00012B/260